Authoritarian Populism and Bovine Political Economy in Modi's India

Authoritarian Populism and Bovine Political Economy in Modi's India analyses how the twin forces of Hindu nationalism and neoliberalism unfold in India's bovine economy, revealing their often-devastating material and economic impact on the country's poor.

This book is a rare, in-depth study of India's bovine economy under Narendra Modi's authoritarian populism. This is an economy that throws up a central paradox: On the one hand, an entrenched and aggressive Hindu nationalist politics is engaged in violently protecting the cow, disciplining those who do not sufficiently respect and revere it; on the other hand, India houses and continuously promotes one of the world's largest corporate-controlled beef export economies that depends on the slaughter of millions of bovines every year. The book offers an original analysis of this scenario to show how Modi's authoritarian populist regime has worked to reconcile the two by simultaneously promoting a virulent Hindu nationalism that seeks to turn India into a Hindu state, while also pushing neoliberal economic policies favouring corporate capital and elite class interests within and beyond the bovine economy.

The book brings out the adverse impacts of these political-economic processes on the lives and livelihoods of millions of poor Indians in countryside and city. In addition, it identifies emerging weaknesses in Modi's authoritarian populism, highlighting the potential for progressive counter-mobilisation. It will be of interest to scholars in the fields of development studies, South Asia studies, critical agrarian studies, as well as scholars with a general interest in political economy, contemporary authoritarian populism, and social movements.

Jostein Jakobsen is a post-doctoral researcher at the Centre for Development and the Environment, University of Oslo, Norway. His research interests are broadly within political ecology and critical agrarian studies. He is the co-author of *The Violent Technologies of Extraction: Political Ecology, Critical Agrarian Studies and the Capitalist Worldeater* (2020).

Kenneth Bo Nielsen is associate professor of social anthropology, University of Oslo, Norway. He works on land politics, agrarian issues, and the political economy of development in India. His books include *Land Dispossession and Everyday Politics in Rural Eastern India* (2018) and *The Great Goa Land Grab* (2022, co-authored).

Routledge Studies in South Asian Politics

36 **Extremism and Counter-Extremism Narratives in Pakistan**
An analysis of narrative building
Sadia Nasir

37 **Politics of Socio-Spatial Transformation in Pakistan**
Leaders and Constituents in Punjab
Asad ur Rehman

38 **Insurgency in India's Northeast**
Identity Formation, Postcolonial Nation/State-Building, and Secessionist Resistance
Jugdep S. Chima and Pahi Saikia

39 **Security of the China Pakistan Economic Corridor**
Counterinsurgency in Balochistan
Khurram Shahzad Siddiqui

40 **Track Two Diplomacy Between India and Pakistan**
Peace Negotiations and Initiatives
Samir Ahmad

41 **Administration in India**
Challenges and Innovations
Edited by Ashish Kumar Srivastava and Iva Ashish Srivastava

42 **Authoritarian Populism and Bovine Political Economy in Modi's India**
Jostein Jakobsen and Kenneth Bo Nielsen

For more information about this series, please visit: www.routledge.com/asianstudies/series/RSSAP

Authoritarian Populism and Bovine Political Economy in Modi's India

Jostein Jakobsen and
Kenneth Bo Nielsen

LONDON AND NEW YORK

First published 2024
by Routledge
4 Park Square, Milton Park, Abingdon, Oxon OX14 4RN

and by Routledge
605 Third Avenue, New York, NY 10158

Routledge is an imprint of the Taylor & Francis Group, an informa business

© 2024 Jostein Jakobsen and Kenneth Bo Nielsen

The right of Jostein Jakobsen and Kenneth Bo Nielsen to be identified as the authors of this work has been asserted in accordance with sections 77 and 78 of the Copyright, Designs and Patents Act 1988.

All rights reserved. No part of this book may be reprinted or reproduced or utilised in any form or by any electronic, mechanical, or other means, now known or hereafter invented, including photocopying and recording, or in any information storage or retrieval system, without permission in writing from the publishers.

Trademark notice: Product or corporate names may be trademarks or registered trademarks, and are used only for identification and explanation without intent to infringe.

British Library Cataloguing-in-Publication Data
A catalogue record for this book is available from the British Library

ISBN: 978-1-032-70934-5 (hbk)
ISBN: 978-1-032-70937-6 (pbk)
ISBN: 978-1-032-70940-6 (ebk)

DOI: 10.4324/9781032709406

Typeset in Times New Roman
by codeMantra

Contents

	List of figures	*vii*
	Acknowledgements	*ix*
1	Authoritarian Populism, Bovines, and State Contradictions in Modi's India	1
2	Hindu Nationalism and Bovine Political Economy	24
3	The "Double Victimisation" of Classes of Labour in Countryside and City	46
4	Towards Corporate Concentration: COVID-19 and Beyond	65
5	Concluding Reflections on State Contradictions and Counter-Hegemonic Projects Under Modi's Authoritarian Populism	84
	Index	*97*

Figures

2.1   India's buffalo meat exports: Quantity in tonnes (MT)   34

Acknowledgements

The authors would like to thank our good colleagues at the University of Oslo's Centre for Development and the Environment (SUM) Arve Hansen and Karen Lykke, whose invitation some five years ago to contribute to a book on meat cultures first brought us together to jointly think about the relationship between bovines, Hindu nationalism, and neoliberalisation in contemporary India. Had it not been for their invitation, this book would not have happened.

Draft chapters have been presented at various workshops and conferences over the past three years. We are grateful for the many constructive comments we have received along the way, and wish to thank Jens Lerche, Richard Axelby, and James Staples, in particular. Their contributions to our conference panel on "Bovine Politics and Agrarian Change: Hindutva, Violence and the Indian Cattle Economy" at the Madison South Asia Conference in 2021 have been particularly influential in shaping our arguments. Thanks also to our regular partner in crime Alf Nilsen for critical input and encouragement; to the Oslo-based South Asia Symposium for the generous discussion of earlier drafts; to the two anonymous reviewers who read the draft manuscript and offered crucial input that helped us reframe the analysis in important ways; and to Sagari Ramdas whose work we remain indebted to, for accepting our invitation to speak on several of the topics discussed in this book at the Norwegian Network for Asian Studies online "Asia Week Conference" in 2020.

We are particularly grateful to Jonathan Pattenden at the *Journal of Agrarian Change*, whose incisive comments and suggestions spawned critical reflections on our part on the scope for progressive counter-movements from below at the current conjuncture. Some material in this book has earlier appeared in article form (Jakobsen and Nielsen 2023) in a special issue of *Journal of Agrarian Change* on "Populism, Agrarian Movements and

Progressive Politics" that Jon guest edited. We are grateful to Taylor and Francis for allowing us to reuse this material here. And, not least, we are grateful to Dorothea Schaefter and Routledge for their work on the book. Part of the research undertaken for the book was carried out under the research project "Transcendence and Sustainability: Asian Visions with Global Promise" (Transsustain), funded by the Research Council of Norway (project number 301352).

Reference

Jakobsen, J., and Nielsen, K. B. 2023. Bovine Meat, Authoritarian Populism, and State Contradictions in Modi's India. *Journal of Agrarian Change* 23 (1): 110–130.

1 Authoritarian Populism, Bovines, and State Contradictions in Modi's India

In March 2016, two Muslim cattle herders were brutally murdered in Balumath in Latehar district in the Indian state of Jharkhand. The deceased were Mazlum Ansari, aged 35, and Imteyaz Khan, aged 12. The two had been herding their last batch of eight oxen to a Friday cattle fair in Chatra district in Jharkhand, where they planned to sell them. Earlier, Mazlum and Imteyaz had reportedly been threatened several times by so-called "cow protection" activists affiliated with a Hindu nationalist right-wing group who had come to Mazlum's house, warning him to stop trading cattle. If he did not, they would kill him. Fearful of his life and business, Mazlum therefore now planned to sell off his last animals and venture into another business. But Mazlum and Imteyaz never made it to the cattle fair. Having set off before sunrise, they were soon intercepted and attacked by a group of cow protection vigilantes in the early hours of the morning. Mazlum and Imteyaz had been forcibly taken to a nearby forest, where they were brutally beaten to death and subsequently hanged from a tree, their hands tied behind their backs, and their eyes covered by cloth. Their bodies were badly bruised, with wounds and injuries inflicted by long, hard, blunt rod-like objects. Imteyaz's father, Azad, had gotten word of the attack and had set out on his motorbike to look for his son. Finding Mazlum's oxen wandering unattended near the road, Azad had heard his son screaming for help from the forest nearby. As he moved towards the forest, Azad had seen the lynch mob and witnessed the attack, but fearing for his own life, he had remained hidden in the bushes: "If I stepped out, they would have killed me too. My son was screaming for help, but I was so scared", he said later (Anwar 2018; HRW 2019).

*

Fifteen months later, in June 2017, Allanasons Pvt. Ltd., India's largest exporter of buffalo meat, received what one commentator called "a remarkable official recognition of the firm's performance", namely a government award for outstanding export performance. Allanasons was one of only two firms that won a so-called diamond trophy, awarded by India's Agricultural and Processed Food Products Export Development Authority (APEDA), the

Commerce Ministry's apex body for agricultural exports. According to an APEDA press release, Allanasons received the award for "outstanding export performance and overall contribution in the food sector" for the years 2014–2015 and 2015–2016. Rita Teotia, the Commerce Secretary in the Narendra Modi-led Hindu nationalist government, observed at the awards function that India was the seventh largest exporter of agricultural products in the world, adding that her ministry was taking steps for "furthering outward shipments". When receiving the award, the Director of Allanasons said that in both years the company had exported buffalo meat at a total value of INR 10,000 crore, amounting to more than one-third of all of India's buffalo meat exports (Dhara 2017). At the same award function, the Aligarh-based Al-Hamd Agro Foods Products Pvt. Ltd. – another major actor exporting halal fresh and frozen buffalo boneless meat and other meat products – was awarded a Golden Trophy for their performance in buffalo meat exports.

*

As the anthropologist James Staples (2020: 7) has recently argued, "beef and the animals from which it comes ... tell us something about what is going on in Indian society in more explicit ways than might otherwise be obvious". In this book, we take inspiration from Staples' argument as we use beef and bovine bodies as our entry point for analysing the political economy of "Modi's India" (Jaffrelot 2021). In this regard, our opening vignettes illustrate two defining and intertwined features or "moments" of what we in this book conceptualise as Modi's authoritarian populism. In the political sphere, we see an aggressively advancing Hindu nationalist cultural politics centred on Hindu pride and unity. This cultural politics seeks (so far with remarkable success) to incorporate significant proportions of India's poor and working classes across the lines of class and caste, in antagonistic opposition to a threatening Muslim "Other" (Jaffrelot 2019, 2021). Bovine bodies are crucial to advancing this agenda, as seen in the way in which Hindu nationalist vigilante groups operate with an increasingly free hand to violently enforce their brand of cow protectionism to punish individuals (and Muslims, in particular) who do not respect the rules of Hindu cow veneration that are upheld as the ultimate indicator of true patriotism (Patel 2018). These groups operate with the tacit approval of the Modi-led Bharatiya Janata Party (BJP) government that has, additionally, presided over the introduction of ever-stricter legal restrictions on the consumption of cow meat and the transportation of cattle for slaughter since it came to power in 2014.

In the economic sphere, however, we find the Modi government heavily invested in neoliberalising the economy, opening up new spaces for capital accumulation by promoting corporate-led agricultural exports from India on a global scale, and extending official awards, recognition, and accolades to central actors in this field. Bovine bodies are crucial to advancing this agenda too as the slaughter of millions of bovines every year is required for key firms in the corporate beef export industry to sell Indian beef meat worth several billion US dollars to markets in the Middle East and South and South-East Asia. These firms are based on corporate concentration around dominant class interests and have been key in establishing India as a world-leading exporter of beef, accounting for as much as 20 percent of global exports.

This scenario has sometimes been discussed in the media and elsewhere as India's "bovine paradox": How is it that India can rigorously "protect the cow" at home while simultaneously killing millions of bovines every year for global exports? While this may at one level seem paradoxical, it is our central contention in this book that India's bovine paradox should be understood as exemplary of broader and acutely important political-economic dynamics and contradictions at play in Modi's India. In schematic form, a central contradiction runs between a bovine *politics* that protects bovine bodies to further the project of "Hindutva ultranationalism" (Kumbamu 2020), and a bovine *economics* that slaughters bovines in the millions to facilitate the further integration of Indian agriculture into global markets and value chains; and between a *political* project that seeks legitimacy from and the incorporation of India's poor and working classes, and an *economic* project that is hostile to the class interests of those same groups. In other words, it runs between the socio-cultural agenda of Hindu nationalist politics and the economic agenda of neoliberal restructuring, both of which are crucially intertwined moments of Modi's authoritarian populism.

Understanding this contradiction and its political-economic dynamics is important in its own right. Indeed, while the unfolding *political* dynamics of Modi's authoritarian populism have been the subject of incisive recent analyses (e.g. Chatterji, Hansen, and Jaffrelot 2019; Hansen and Roy 2022; Jaffrelot 2021), the political economy of the Modi regime remains "secretive" (Jaffrelot 2021: 459) and underexplored. This book seeks to address this lacuna by bringing *economic* relations of production into central consideration to understand the form and direction of capital accumulation in Modi's India. Drawing on Nicos Poulantzas' notion of "state contractions", which we return to below, a key aim in this book is therefore to illuminate and understand capitalist dynamics under Modi's authoritarian populism, using India's bovine paradox as our entry point and magnifying glass.

An important related aim is to understand the wider ramifications of these dynamics and contradictions as they unfold in the specific domain of bovines for the hundreds of millions of rural Indians who live precarious lives in the Indian countryside. This is a heterogeneous category that we in this book conceptualise as rural "classes of labour", that is, "all those who share a position as members of directly and indirectly exploited classes" (Pattenden 2023: 6). India has the highest livestock population in the world, at more than half a billion animals. Of these, more than 300 million are bovines, making rural Indians the largest global owners of this species (Narayanan 2023: 15–16). Given the average size of a rural Indian household, coupled with the fact that the mean "herd size" of bovines in rural India is just one or two animals, it is clear that the bovine economy is important to a very large number of rural Indians. Indeed, approximately two-thirds of all rural households report generating income from livestock (Mahapatra 2012). Already a decade ago, livestock surpassed crop production in terms of monetary contribution to the Indian economy (Mahapatra 2012), and more than a quarter of the total earnings in the category known as "agriculture and allied activities" now comes from livestock (Narayanan 2023: 11). These additionally act as an important "living bank" for rural households who increasingly have to manoeuvre a situation of agrarian distress and economic hardships. Changes to the bovine political economy, in other words, very directly and very immediately impact the lives and livelihoods of India's classes of labour in rural but also "rurban" and urban areas, where bovines are important to the livelihoods of cattle traders, transporters, butchers, tanners, leatherworkers, craftsmen, and small retailers in the informal economy.

A key argument of this book is that the ways in which central contradictions in Modi's authoritarian populism have played out in the domain of bovine politics and economics have had distinctly negative ramifications for India's classes of labour. Specifically, we show how those groups among classes of labour in the countryside and cities across India whose livelihoods are dependent upon the livestock economy have, in various ways, experienced a "double victimisation", being at the receiving end of destructive Hindu nationalist cow vigilantism and legal crackdowns, as well as at the losing end of an ongoing restructuring of the livestock economy that favours major actors backed and represented by dominant class interests. What our story shows, then, is that ongoing Hindu nationalist efforts at incorporating India's poor and working classes in their political project notwithstanding, the bovine politics and economics of the Modi regime offer few benefits for India's classes of labour. They are, rather, destructive of key parts of the livelihoods of these groups and overwhelmingly further accumulation among politically favoured classes of corporate capital. A final aim of this book is, therefore, to use this finding to reflect on the extent to which these political-economic dynamics constitute a potential challenge to the longer-term reproduction of Modi's authoritarian populist regime. To what extent can the Modi regime sustain what Echeverri-Gent and colleagues (2021: 425) call the paradox of "remarkable political success amidst serious economic distress"? Leaning towards the optimism of the will rather than the pessimism of the intellect, this book uses the analysis of bovine political economy under Modi to explore openings or possibilities for political unravelling that may pave the way for novel forms of counter-hegemonic mobilisation from below.

In the remainder of this introductory chapter, we introduce the key themes and analytical concepts that run through the book. We start with a brief review of the literature on bovines and India's bovine paradox, before situating our analysis in an emerging literature within critical agrarian studies scrutinising the relationship between authoritarian populism and the rural world. We then mobilise the idea of "state contradictions" to analyse the political economy of the Modi regime in general terms and elaborate on our argument about its key contradictions. We end with an overview of the chapters followed by a note on methodology.

The Bovine Paradox, Authoritarian Populism, and State Contradictions

India's seeming bovine paradox has been the subject of discussions in the media from time to time, especially since the news broke in 2015 that India had by then emerged as the world's leading exporter of beef meat in the form of carabeef, that is, meat from water buffaloes. Commentators taking a critical stance against Hindu nationalism have often pointed to this paradox, where the BJP and affiliated Hindu right-wing groups target beef and meat consumption at home while encouraging their exports abroad, as evidence of hypocrisy and the cynical readiness on the part of the government to discard the mask of Hindu piety and cow veneration in favour of export revenue.

The still relatively limited scholarly literature that has substantially engaged with this bovine paradox has, in contrast, sought to move beyond the often intensely polarising debates that "the hyper-politicization of beef" (Narayanan 2023: 9) can generate, to probe deeper complexities and nuances. Recent contributions from the anthropology of food, such as Staples' (2020) *Sacred Cows and Chicken Manchurian: The Everyday Politics of Eating Meat in India* and Johan Fischer's (2023) *Vegetarianism, Meat and Modernity in India*, illustrate convincingly the often marginal or contradictory effects that broader discourses on Hindu nationalism, cow protectionism, and "beef bans" have on people's everyday foodways and culinary choices, foregrounding instead how the latter are shaped by a wider set of social and economic processes. Other scholars have approached the paradox from the standpoint of interspecies or multispecies ethnography and animal studies. Radhika Govindrajan's *Animal Intimacies: Interspecies Relatedness in India's Central Himalayas* (2018) provides an ethnographically grounded analysis of the limits to the Hindu nationalist project of cow protectionism by showing how its use of undifferentiated and abstract metaphors of the cow as mother of the Hindu nation is disrupted by "the distinct and lively materiality of the actual cows it [seeks] to represent" (Govindrajan 2018: 65, emphasis in original), and by people's embodied everyday relationships with real bovines of flesh, blood, and emotion. From a comparable starting point, Adcock and Govindrajan's (2019) collection "Bovine Politics in South Asia: Rethinking Religion, Law and Ethics" similarly seeks to move the discussion of India's bovines beyond questions of politicised religion by attending to the materialities of bovine-human interactions and how bovines co-produce social worlds with humans. In doing so, they persuasively deconstruct many of the misleading binaries that both inform but also blur the discussion of bovines in India: The holy cow vs. the merely economic buffalo; legality vs. illegality; and ethical living vs. violent practices. Equally firmly rooted in the same multispecies tradition, Yamini Narayanan's (2023) *Mother Cow, Mother India: A Multispecies Politics of Dairy in India* offers a powerful critique of the way in which current Indian debates on the cow have become so polarised and hyperpoliticised that the animal itself is almost lost from view. In recuperating the bodily experience of bovines in the Indian dairy and meat industry, Narayanan brings to our attention another paradox that the strong focus on cow protectionism in the context of slaughter and beef exports glosses over, namely that while the slaughter of bovines is intensely politicised by Hindu nationalist organisations for whom the Mother cow embodies Mother India, the routine, large-scale violence done to bovine bodies in the Indian dairy industry – culminating in slaughter when animals are "spent" or "superfluous" – is whitewashed almost to the point of complete erasure.

These studies have opened important new avenues for exploring the roles and relationships that are formed around bovines in India and have crucially shifted the terms of scholarly engagement away from rigid binary conceptions. We draw inspiration from and engage with these studies throughout the book. And yet, our interest in using India's bovine paradox as an entry point for understanding the political economy of the Modi regime and its consequences for India's rural classes of labour necessarily requires a closer engagement with the growing literature on authoritarian populism. This is a literature in which India has come to figure ever more prominently over the past decade, as the country's democratic institutions have withered, and its political leadership turned increasingly autocratic under Modi's Hindu nationalist government. The various strands of this literature commonly conceptualise Modi as a "national populist" (Jaffrelot 2021) or an "authoritarian populist" (Chacko 2018; Nielsen and Nilsen 2022a; Sinha 2021; Sud 2022) and point to the same two defining features of this form of politics that we outlined above, namely (i) an aggressive and assertive religious nationalism that seeks to turn India into a Hindu majoritarian state (Chatterji, Hansen and Jaffrelot 2019; Jaffrelot 2021; Hansen and Roy 2022), and (ii) neoliberal economic policies that seek to remove obstacles to and create new spaces for capitalist accumulation (Kaur 2020; Palshikar 2019). In this sense, Modi's authoritarian populism has much in common with that of Erdogan in Turkey (Adaman and Akbulut 2021), Trump in the USA (Kellner 2016), Bolsonaro in Brazil (Tamaki, Mendonça and Fereira 2021), and Duterte in the Philippines (Juego 2017; Ruud 2023), who all combine an exclusionary nationalism with neoliberal restructuring of the state and economy. Indeed, given the entrenchment and hegemonic consolidation of the Modi regime (Bello 2019), Modi has come to be seen as an almost paradigmatic example of the rise of new authoritarian populisms in both established and emerging democracies across the Global North and South (Widmalm 2021). This new wave of "democratic backsliding" may be unfolding in a slow and piecemeal way, but it has affected a very high number of democracies across the globe (Berberoglu 2020; Lührmann et al. 2018), including the world's largest democracy, India.

The main contributions to the study of the relationship between authoritarian populism and the rural world that is among our key interests here have, however, come from the field of critical agrarian studies where the topic has received unprecedented attention in recent years. This is largely due to the research emanating from the Emancipatory Rural Politics Initiative, a collaborative effort among scholars and activists striving to unravel the ramification for rural politics of right-wing deepening across the world.[1] The Emancipatory Rural Politics Initiative has spawned a series of publications scrutinising this relationship under various concepts such as "authoritarian populism" (Scoones et al. 2018), "counter-revolution" (Bello 2019), "right-wing populism" (Borras 2020; Pattenden 2023), or "reactionary nationalist populisms" (Akram-Lodhi 2022). While this scholarship acknowledges variegation in actually existing forms and dynamics across different parts of the Global South and North alike, recognising the academic and political pitfalls of over-extending the reach of a singular analytic, these various concepts all index a defining political feature of populism, namely "the deliberate political act of aggregating disparate and even competing and contradictory class and group interests and demands into a relatively homogenised voice, that is, 'we, the people', against an 'adversarial them' for tactical or strategic purposes" (Borras 2020: 5). Such political dynamics, the literature argues, need to be seen in relation to how authoritarian populisms take shape in rural societies, drawing upon ongoing processes of economic and social change, for the most part contributing to worsening and deepening economic dynamics that are detrimental to rural classes of labour (Scoones et al. 2018). These dynamics – all of which are on display in contemporary India – include widespread and longstanding yet accelerating conditions of distress, resource grabbing, widening rural-urban disparities, environmental breakdown, and agro-industrial transformation that are largely unhinged from employment generation or other economic benefits to rural communities and classes of labour. This is coupled with a likewise widespread exhaustion of progressive counter-mobilisation in much of the world (Scoones et al. 2018). In other words, the rise of authoritarian populism in the rural world – in India and elsewhere – simultaneously indexes an increasingly generalised crisis *and* a dire need for emancipatory politics from below (see also Pattenden 2023).

Despite the clear acknowledgement of the intertwined nature of the political and economic "moments" of authoritarian populism, much of the recent scholarship on authoritarian populism and the rural world has retained a primary interest in the ideological and discursive qualities of authoritarian populism. This has, in turn, triggered new interventions calling for a recalibration of analytical emphasis towards more in-depth and sustained probing of constitutive capitalist and class dynamics. Henry Bernstein (2020: 1539), for example, writes that: "What should be clear enough is that authoritarian populism, for all its diverse manifestations, should always be interrogated first through the questions: what class interests does it serve? By what means? And with what effects?" Taking a cue from Bernstein's assessment, McKay and colleagues similarly argue for moving beyond analysing authoritarian populism in a solely discursive manner, to probe underlying capitalist dynamics that structure authoritarian populism, with their distinctive class contradictions and antagonisms. This, they write, "requires going beyond the discourse to a serious engagement with the role and nature of the state, and thus, an analysis into the nature of the class and intra-class relationships in society and in agrarian formation" (McKay et al. 2020: 355).

In this book, we are inspired by this call for shifting the study of authoritarian populism from the domain of ideology and discourse, into the domain of the state, capitalist dynamics, and class and intra-class relationships. By exploring Bernstein's questions of what class interests authoritarian populism serves, by what means, and with what effects in the specific context of India's bovine paradox, we seek to shed new light on the political economy of the Modi regime, and on the transformations this regime is bringing about. We do so through an engagement with the writings of Nicos Poulantzas, whose work in the Gramscian tradition (Gramsci 1971) on "authoritarian statism" inspired Stuart Hall's original thinking on authoritarian populism in the context of Thatcherism in Britain (Hall 2011: 727–728; McKay et al. 2020). We suggest, however, that the call for renewed attention to the state to unravel the capitalist dynamic beneath right-wing populism across the world invites attention to another strand of Poulantzas' writings: his idea of "state contradictions". Poulantzas (1978) discusses the state as "a relationship of forces, or more precisely the material condensation of such a relationship among classes and class fractions" (ibid.: 128, emphasis removed). This relationship is necessarily strained and frequently conflictual, giving rise to a series of "internal contradictions within the State" (ibid., emphasis removed). Therefore, rather than looking for contradictions in hegemonies as such, or in hegemonic projects, Poulantzas offers a perspective that would emphasise contradictions within the state – within, in the Indian case, a state housing an authoritarian populism constituted by Hindu nationalist politics and neoliberal economics. Importantly, Poulantzas' class-analytical approach to the state also invites consideration of the conjuncturally specific articulations between the "political" and the "economic", considered not as distinct realms, but rather as aspects or "moments" of capitalist constellations, where relations of production – comprising both "political" class relations and "economic" relations – always remain determinant (Poulantzas 2008: 396–397).

While Poulantzas' class-analytical focus has been critiqued for underplaying the "economic" and for paying "too little attention ... to basing the analysis of class struggle on the actual dynamic of capital accumulation" (Holloway and Picciotto 1978: 9),[2] we find the Poulantzasian lens fruitful for scrutinising the ways in which state contradictions play out across the ostensibly "political" and "economic" aspects of Modi's authoritarian populism. Insisting with Simon Clarke (1991: 9) that "the economic, political and ideological are complementary forms of a single social relation" under capitalism and the ubiquitous compulsions of the capital-labour relation, in what follows we draw on the suggestive formulation of state contradictions – seen as aspects of the patterning of "the fundamental class antagonism of capital and labour" (Bonefeld 1992: 107) – to analyse Modi's authoritarian populism and its central contradictions. Consequently, we argue, rethinking authoritarian populism – in contemporary India as well as elsewhere – to explore state and class relations underpinning the ideological or discursive realm demands a careful and simultaneous engagement with accumulation dynamics *and* their contradictions.

State Contradictions in Modi's India: Neoliberalisation and Accumulation Patterns

To grasp state contradictions in Modi's India, we proceed from the observation that the growth model pursued by the BJP – and indeed by all Indian governments since economic liberalisation gathered momentum in 1991 – has been highly unequal in its economic impact, generating stark social and economic inequities (Drèze and Sen 2013). Importantly, these inequities have increased since the Modi government assumed office in 2014, with estimates by Chancel and Piketty (2019) suggesting that inequality has now reached its highest level since the days of the British Raj.[3] This is evident in the strong increase in the number of Indian dollar billionaires in the last few years, and the fact that the richest 98 of these own the same amount of wealth as the 555 million people who make up the poorest 40 percent of the Indian population (Oxfam India 2022: 7).

To appreciate how the Modi regime's brand of neoliberalism builds on and departs from that of its predecessors, it is instructive to briefly contextualise it with reference to the longer Indian experience with liberalising economic reforms since the early 1990s. In contrast to many countries in Latin America and Africa, India never experienced the kind of neoliberal shock therapy that came with structural adjustment programmes. Rather, the reforms that India undertook from the early 1990s and into the early 2000s were carried out "by stealth" (Jenkins 1999). As Nielsen and Nilsen (2022b) have argued, this early period of restructuring can be understood as a form of incremental roll-back neoliberalisation, focused on selective deregulation and gradual state-led marketisation. The pace of neoliberal reform only picked up momentum under a

BJP-led government (Corbridge and Harriss 2000) in the late 1990s. The BJP government branded their neoliberal reforms under the sign of "India Shining", upholding these as the prime strategy of social mobility and prosperity in India (Kaur 2020: 125). However, as it became increasingly clear that these reforms had produced neither high economic growth, nor social mobility and prosperity for most Indians, simmering popular opposition to neoliberalism eventually led to a change of government in 2004.

While the Congress-led coalition – the United Progressive Alliance (UPA) – that replaced the BJP largely remained committed to maintaining and even deepening the process of neoliberal restructuring,[4] it was also compelled to respond to countervailing social forces to shore up popular legitimacy and negotiate the required consent to govern in the context of competitive democratic politics. Towards this end, the UPA formulated a political programme that sought to address the needs of India's poor masses and classes of labour in the countryside (see Hasan 2012; Nilsen 2021). This programme entailed the rolling out of a series of social policy interventions in the form of rights-based legislation that aimed to mitigate the marginalisation of vulnerable groups that neoliberalisation invariably produced (Ruparelia 2013). The interventions included new and ambitious welfare programmes in employment, food security, and education – programmes which, despite their uneven and often patchy implementation, became important to the lives of millions of rural Indians. The UPA's rights-based approach to social policy in many ways, then, represented a partial and contradictory move in the direction of roll-out neoliberalism that combines regulatory reform with active state-building and the disciplining and containment of those marginalised by earlier waves of roll-back neoliberalism (Peck and Tickell 2002). In this sense, the UPA years most clearly brought to light the "contradiction of the simultaneous production of neoliberal and welfare policy" (Ahmed and Chatterjee 2016: 332) in India.

Up until the end of the UPA period, then, neoliberalisation in India had been restrained, incomplete, and contradictory, even as the overall thrust was towards opening ever-more sectors to private capital, creating new avenues for accumulation for corporate and dominant class interests (Chatterjee 2008; Gupta and Sivaramakrishnan 2011). By 2014, however, the UPA project had unravelled. An important driver of this change was the fact that Indian capital had, in the years leading up to the crucial 2014 elections that brought Modi to power, more or less unanimously fallen in line behind Modi and the BJP. This shift was propelled in large part by dissatisfaction with the UPA's roll-out of rights-based welfare which India's capitalists had come to regard as a wasteful drain on the state exchequer (Desai 2016: 53). As Kothakapa and Sirohi (2023: 14–15) put it, top corporates criticised the return of "socialism" under the UPA while the middle classes decried what they saw as freebies for the poor. Corporate India massively funded Modi's 2014 campaign, leading commentators on the left to describe the elections as "the biggest corporate heist in history".

With the subsequent coming to power of the authoritarian populist Modi government, India has seen a departure from the inclusive, incremental "rollout neoliberalism" of the UPA towards a more unambiguous promotion of pro-business policies. In the political sphere, this has been accompanied by a shift from the moderately secular orientation of the prior government, towards a more assertive form of Hindu nationalism that seeks to render India a Hindu state,[5] advancing through the kind of violent xenophobia and racism that characterise authoritarian populisms more generally (Borras 2020). Indeed, these two features or "moments" – economic neoliberalism and political Hindu nationalism – are, as we have argued, constitutive of Modi's authoritarian populism. To appreciate how this authoritarian populism works across these "moments", it is worth quoting extensively from Suhas Palshikar's illuminating work on the BJP's strategy for "crafting a new hegemony" under Modi:

> What the Modi regime is set to do is to acquire the support of corporate interests separately (i.e., unconnected from the cultural agenda) for its *economic* agenda, and at the same time, acquire approval for its *socio-political* agenda from the larger public by linking it to the economic agenda. The corporate classes are expected not to be interested in or concerned with the emerging debates in the arena of public political culture believing that irrespective of what political culture emerges, the *economic* agenda would be implemented vigorously and the erosion of diversity would not hurt the material interests of the corporates. On the other hand, the ordinary citizen is sought to be convinced that economic wellbeing is primarily a function of a strong nation and therefore, the hurdles in becoming a strong nation (such as social schisms, minority appeasement, anti-national use of freedom of expression) need to be overcome. This is where the ability of Modi to bring together the middle classes and corporate interests become crucial. This alliance is critical not only to his electoral prospects, but more so for the hegemonic project. Modi emerges as the extraordinary leader because of skilfully marrying an aggressive corporatized economy with an assertive majoritarian politics.
>
> (Palshikar 2019: 113–114, emphasis added)

As Ravinder Kaur (2020) has shown, Modi's work on forging this crucial close alignment between Hindu nationalist majoritarianism and an aggressive neoliberalisation of the economy goes back to the early 2000s when he was Chief Minister of the state of Gujarat. While the story of the crafting of Modi's image as an "extraordinary leader" and iconic enabler of corporate-led economic growth and development has been told (and deconstructed) elsewhere (e.g. Jaffrelot 2021; Muraleedharan 2023; Sud 2022), what is important for our purposes is the considerable degree of success Modi has had in articulating and building consent around his authoritarian populist project that marries Hindu nationalist politics with neoliberal economics. As Shankar Gopalakrishnan (2006, 2009) has argued, there are strong resonances and overlaps between the ideology of Hindu nationalism and the ideology of neoliberalism, and the alliance between the two has grown gradually, albeit at times uneasily, since the 1990s. Yet only with the ascent of Modi has this alliance successfully consolidated into a singular hegemonic project. Under Modi, Kaur argues, neoliberalisation is mediated by a cultural politics centred on "the desire to unhinge the national from its colonial past and the impatience to inhabit the long-promised future" (Kaur 2020: 18). The new nation that is to emerge from this, Kaur writes, is partly a capitalist dreamworld in which investor-citizens can enjoy social mobility and material prosperity. But it is also "an ancient Hindu civilizational culture that assumes new forms but never loses its original essence" (ibid.: 109). This ideology is then fused with accumulation strategies that bear the imprint of Modi's close relationship with big business. As Palshikar also observes, Modi has been so instrumental in creating and holding together this fusion that he now embodies "the entanglements between the imperatives of capitalist growth and ... cultural nationalism" (Kaur 2020: 248). In contrast to the lacklustre and largely unsuccessful "India Shining" campaign of the previous BJP government, then, Modi has been much more successful in harnessing the dream of "good times" to the vehicle of Hindu nationalism, instrumentalising the neoliberal formula of economic growth towards the making of a strong Hindu nation. This, Kaur argues (2020: 246), locks "illiberal" cultural nationalism and "neoliberal" capitalist growth into a state of mutual indebtedness under authoritarian populist leadership.

Yet as Palshikar's remark on the "aggressive corporatized economy" under Modi indicates,[6] the current trajectory is one where major capitals and specific capitalists – especially those on friendly terms with Modi's regime (Banaji 2022; Jaffrelot 2021) – are put in an increasingly comfortable position within the evolving political economy, driving increasing concentration of ownership across a range of industries (Chandra 2020; Chandra and Verma 2020). An estimate from 2023 found that a mere 20 companies accounted for a full 80 percent of India Inc's total earnings, up from around 70 percent in 2019. The corresponding figure for early 2014 just before Modi came to power was less than 40 percent. In 1989, just prior to the commencement of liberalising economic reforms, the figure was a mere 14 percent (Jaffrelot 2021; Rajhansa and Mukherjea 2023). This accelerating drive towards greater corporate concentration tallies with Kothakapa and Sirohi's (2023) recent assessment that dominant fractions of capital have enjoyed unprecedented opportunities to entrench their power and wealth during the years when Modi has been prime minister. During this period, the largest and most profitable firms have been winning out disproportionately, while small capitalists, in contrast, find themselves increasingly marginalised. This, in turn, has fuelled speculations that India may be moving towards a new form of "conglomerate" capitalism dominated by a small number of large firms (Damodaran 2020), or a new and increasingly unstable "oligarchic state capitalism" characterised by "incestuously close links between state and business" (Chatterjee 2023; see also Sircar 2022).

Crucial to our analysis, these political-economic developments have been accompanied by a depression of macro-economic indicators under Modi, alongside declining growth rates and increasing levels of hunger (Kothakapa and Sirohi 2023) – all indicators of the precarious situation that India's classes of labour are facing. Indeed, unemployment in India is currently at its highest level since the 1990s and exceeds those of most other emerging economies in the Global South (Nilsen 2023), with youth unemployment, in particular, being "shockingly high" (Basu, cited in Subramaniam and Farooqui 2023). The real wages for workers engaged in construction work, or as agricultural labourers or non-agricultural workers have remained almost stagnant since Modi came to power, growing by less than 1 percent per year, thus indexing a real crisis for India's classes of labour. This crisis is mirrored in poverty estimates. While no new government data on poverty has been published while Modi has been in power, World Bank estimates from 2019 suggested that close to 45 percent of all Indians lived on less than USD 3.65 per day. In all, the poorest half of the Indian population – around 700 million people – now earns just 13 percent of all national income and owns only 6 percent of the national wealth (Nilsen 2023). Unsurprisingly, this precarious situation for India's poor and working classes also registers in the domains of nutrition and hunger: In 2022, India slipped for the third consecutive year in the Global Hunger Index to 107th position among 121 countries – lower than other South Asian countries such as Pakistan, Nepal, Sri Lanka, and Bangladesh – registering significant levels of undernourishment and child stunting in the population (*Al Jazeera* 2022). In Modi's India, in other words, increasing concentration of wealth and power at the top has been accompanied by greater precarity and a crisis of social reproduction among India's classes of labour.

This escalating *economic* instability and vulnerability emanating from the class dynamics of state-capital relations under Modi, Elizabeth Chatterjee (2023) suggest, may render Modi's authoritarian populism *politically* vulnerable. To appreciate how and why, we need to consider how – as the references to the importance of "the larger public" and "the ordinary citizen" in Palshikar's analysis of the BJP's hegemonic strategy – Modi and the BJP actively seek to incorporate and gain political legitimacy from India's poor and working classes. Since 2014, this strategy has met with considerable success as lower caste groups and poor voters have been drawn into the BJP's ambit of electoral support in greater numbers: In 2019, the BJP won 44 percent of the lower caste vote, around a third of the Dalit vote, and 36 percent of the votes of the poor. In all, Modi and the BJP garnered support from 44 percent of all

Hindu voters across the lines of caste and class that are otherwise often salient political identities (Nilsen 2023).

This significant inclusion of classes of labour into the Hindu nationalist support base has been sought and achieved through a complex mix of strategies. Electoral promises of unprecedented economic growth and "good times" for all – backed up by sensationalist accounts of Modi's achievements during his tenure as chief minister of Gujarat – early on tapped into the frustrations and aspirations of both the poor and the moderately upwardly mobile neo-middle classes, predominantly from backward caste backgrounds (Jaffrelot 2015). This has been supplemented by an albeit moderate provision of targeted welfare initiatives whereby *individual* voters are provided with tangible *private* goods such as cooking gas, toilets, and medical insurance, which register more immediately in the lived experience of poorer citizens than do substantial investments in more diffuse public goods such as education and public health (Echeverri-Gent, Sinha and Wyatt 2021). In addition, Modi's authoritarian populist style has played a key role in mobilising support amongst India's classes of labour, projecting him as a strong, committed, and compassionate leader in whom also poor voters can place their trust in exchange for "good decisions for the polity" (Sircar 2020). To this we can add the power of fascination that Hindu nationalism's discourse of Hindu unity and a shared sense of Hinduness has, in some contexts, been shown to exercise vis-à-vis Dalits, who may "seek acceptance from the upper-caste Hindus who had always culturally and socially marginalised them" (Narayan 2009). Alf Nilsen (2023) conceives of this as a form of "psychological wages" that accrue to India's poor and working classes through their involvement in Hindu nationalist politics, extending a promise of dignity, recognition, and development that can only be realised within the Hindu fold. Such psychological wages may be supplemented by what Thomas Blom Hansen (2001) calls "wages of violence". The violence that is integral to contemporary Hindu nationalist politics through, for example, cow protection vigilantism relies on a cohort of "angry young men" (Jaffrelot 2021: 87–89) recruited across castes. They carry out public acts of violence and vandalism, attacks on "anti-national minorities", and the destruction of property, thereby carving open new spaces for the public assertion and affirmation of plebeian or stigmatised identities (Hansen 2001: 61–66).

And yet, the escalating economic instability, the widespread and increasing precarity among India's classes of labour, the prolonged betrayal of the promise of material betterment, and the crisis of social reproduction that emanate from intensifying class dynamics of state-capital relations under Modi's authoritarian populism arguably indicate a space from which the Modi regime may potentially be rendered vulnerable. In our terms, this points most clearly to the acute need, intellectually and politically, for unravelling state contradictions, their concomitant capital and class dynamics, and their on-the-ground

Authoritarian Populism, Bovines, and State Contradictions 15

ramifications as these unfold in Modi's India. The remainder of the book seeks to do this in the realm of India's bovine political economy.

The Structure of the Book and the Argument

We start, in the next chapter, with a comprehensive analysis of the central state contradictions that are at the heart of Modi's authoritarian populism. Starting from an analysis of the politics of vigilantism, cow protectionism, and the weaponisation of "bovine symbolism" (Staples 2020: 12) in Hindu nationalist discourse and practice, the chapter demonstrates the centrality of bovines to the Hindu nationalist project of turning India into a Hindu state. This project, we show, also unfolds in the legal domain where ever-stricter laws have been introduced to simultaneously protect the cow and discipline and punish those who harm her. Central state contradictions, however, become visible when we conjoin the analysis of this political moment of Modi's authoritarian populism to its economic counterpart, revealing a surge in beef exports emanating from an expanding formal meat sector, operating with state support – albeit strained – yet sitting in uneasy proximity to the bovine politics being pursued by Hindu nationalist forces. Using bovines as a lens for exploring and empirically grounding the larger story of neoliberalisation and accumulation patterns in India recounted above, we uncover a process of considerable restructuring of the bovine economy over the last decades, characterised by the expansion and consolidation of a corporate beef export sector dominated by a limited number of large capitalist enterprises. Their rise within the bovine political economy aligns with the overall neoliberalising thrust of the Modi regime and, we argue, entails novel class and accumulation dynamics that differ markedly from how the livestock economy functions within the livelihoods of the country's classes of labour. The emerging scenario is one where an informal bovine economy largely in the hands of classes of labour faces usurping competition from a formal industry that is centralised, capital intensive, and firmly controlled by dominant class interests.

The subsequent chapters further explore the unfolding dynamics of these state contradictions in the realm of the country's bovine political economy. Chapter 3 analyses their impact among classes of labour in the Indian countryside and cities, documenting their decidedly negative consequences. Classes of labour engaged in sectors of the bovine economy across the rural-urban divide, we argue, live through what we refer to as a process of double victimisation. Specific segments of classes of labour are both direct and indirect victims of new forms of legal and extra-legal regulation of the bovine economy that restrict their economic agency and produce economic hardship and physical suffering. At the same time, they are also increasingly excluded from a transforming bovine economy because of broader political-economic restructurings that favour dominant class interests. This chapter thus offers substantial evidence concerning the class interests that Modi's authoritarian populism serves, as well as its ramifications. In addition, the double victimisation of classes of labour explored in this chapter potentially has broader implications for the capacity of Modi's authoritarian populism to successfully seek legitimacy from India's poor and working classes. Irrespective of the fact that the social, economic, and political emaciation of Muslim classes of labour is integral to the political moment of Modi's authoritarian populism, the wider negative impact of this politics on India's complex and extensive bovine economy nevertheless means that the livelihoods of larger segments of India's classes of labour that Modi's regime seeks to incorporate are considerably undermined. The political implications of this are something we return to in the concluding chapter.

Chapter 4 analyses the acceleration and intensification of the political-economic dynamics in the bovine sector analysed in earlier chapters during and immediately after the COVID-19 pandemic. In this period, fast-changing class and accumulation dynamics in the bovine economy have, we argue, enabled further corporate consolidation across multiple sectors. This trajectory of change in favour of elite class interests and large corporate actors, we suggest, means that the organised industry is now increasingly well-positioned to capture a larger share of the value hitherto produced and retained among classes of labour in the informal bovine economy. This, we argue, starkly reveals the underlying class bias of Modi's authoritarian populism. When read alongside the previous chapter's argument that the incorporation of already-precarious classes of labour in Modi's political project increasingly occurs through the destruction of key parts of their livelihoods, this chapter demonstrates how the state contradictions that this book is centrally concerned with are arguably moving towards being *less* contradictory insofar as the political and economic moments of Modi's authoritarian populism move towards increasing alignment in an intensifying manner.

While this emerging dynamic may safely be interpreted as an acute threat to the livelihoods of millions of rural Indians, it also opens for another – and more hopeful – line of thinking politically about the prospects for emancipatory or counter-hegemonic projects. This is the ambition of our concluding chapter. Returning to our central contention that India's "bovine paradox" must be understood as an exemplar of broader political-economic dynamics at play in Modi's India – and of the contradiction between Hindu nationalism's attempts at incorporating India's poor and working classes while also pushing neoliberal economic restructuring to the benefit of capitalist classes – we suggest that the unfolding intensification of such dynamics may index emerging structural conditions of possibility for progressive counter-hegemonic mobilisation. In making this argument, the concluding chapter engages the emerging scholarship on the recent farmers' agitations in India, locating structural conditions of counter-hegemonic mobilisation surrounding bovines within broader dynamics in a restructuring economy in which agrarian relations are taking on novel configurations; and where Modi's authoritarian populism seeks political majority by pitting classes of labour against each other.

A Note on Methodology and Representation

When researching this book, we have worked almost entirely with secondary sources. Both of us have carried out longer and shorter ethnographic fieldworks in different parts of India since the early 2000s, on subjects as diverse as land grabbing, agrarian change, social movements and democracy, the political economy of development, and Hindu nationalist politics. This earlier research forms an important backdrop to how we approach and analyse the material we present in this book. That material, in turn, consists of the extant academic literature, as well as reporting, accounts, and investigations by journalists, social activists, academics, and other actors writing about bovine politics and economics in contemporary India. We also draw on material produced by and on the Indian beef industry, including promotional material, trade statistics, and online self-presentations, in addition to relevant government policy documents.

Locating material on that part of the story which involves Hindu nationalist vigilantism and extra-legal violence was, alarmingly, surprisingly easy. Such atrocities are in no small measure carried out in spectacularly violent form, to intimidate minorities in general and further communal polarisation on a larger scale. It is, in other words, undertaken for public consumption and is meant to be visible. It is sometimes filmed and shared on social media, is widely reported on in the national and international media, and figures prominently in many accounts of contemporary Hindu nationalism.

The part of the story that centres on the political economy of the bovine sector and of the Modi regime, however, proved considerably more difficult to research. This is no doubt attributable to the generally secretive nature of the latter, and to the "sensitive" and sometimes-controversial nature of the former. Our analysis of these factors therefore draws eclectically on a very diverse number of sources, which we seek to piece together into a bigger picture. The same is the case for our account of the impact of Modi's authoritarian populism on rural classes of labour which similarly builds on secondary sources, and which would arguably have been greatly enriched by long-term fieldwork in specific rural settings. We hope readers will take the analysis and arguments in this monograph as an invitation to undertake precisely this.

Since the aim of this relatively short book is to describe and analyse the big picture, a more fine-grained and systematic mapping of interstate variation is beyond the scope of this book. Instead, we draw selectively on empirical examples from several Indian states to illustrate broader trends. A few states, however, receive more in-depth attention, particularly Uttar Pradesh and

Karnataka. Although these states have markedly different demographic, economic, cultural, and linguistic histories and characteristics, they are widely seen as the two most crucial "laboratories of Hindutva" today (Dhingra 2022; Ramakrishnan 2020). In both states, BJP governments have used their control of the state to tighten legal frameworks regulating the transport, slaughter, and consumption of bovines to further the political project of Hindu nationalism, while allied organisations operating in civil society have used extralegal vigilantism to violently regulate the lives, livelihoods, and behaviour of minorities, with the tacit or even active support of state institutions and the police. This fusion of Hindu nationalist forces in political and civil society has been described by Jaffrelot (2021: 250) as constituting "a vigilante state whose ideal type has taken shape in [Chief Minister] Yogi Adityanath's Uttar Pradesh", but which also exists in some form in Karnataka and other states (see also Nielsen, Selvaraj and Nilsen forthcoming). In addition, Uttar Pradesh is a particularly crucial state to any discussion of bovine political economy as it contributes close to two-thirds of India's overall meat export revenues, houses close to half of all abattoirs and meat processing export units in the country, and has the highest buffalo population of any Indian state (Alavi 2020). It is also a state with upwards of 100 million people living under or just above the official poverty line, and where vigilante groups are given a particularly free hand. In Uttar Pradesh, we thus find the most striking manifestations of the processes that we are concerned with in this book: Virulent Hindu nationalist forces, significant parts of India's beef agro-industry, and those sections of rural classes of labour most heavily affected by double victimisation.

Based on this material, the book attempts to tell a singular story, a story that connects and interweaves the lives of small farmers and other owners of bovines in the Indian countryside; cattle traders, dealers, and transporters; butchers, tanners, and leatherworkers; the dairy industry, informal abattoirs, and modernised export-oriented slaughterhouses; cow protection activists, cow shelters, and corporate social responsibility; informal markets and global value chains; and Hindu nationalism and neoliberalism. Each chapter tells one or more parts of this interconnected story.

Notes

1 See https://www.iss.nl/en/research/research-networks/emancipatory-rural-politics-initiative
2 This shortcoming is derived from the "conceptual gulf" (Mau 2023: 56) between the "political" and the "economic" that is taken for granted in his approach, arguably an abiding flaw in much Marxist theorising (see Wood 1995).
3 The exact level of economic inequality in India today is debated. Some recent estimates suggest that it remains high and widening (Nilsen 2023), while others detect a slight decline in inequality since 2019 (Ghatak, Raghavan, and Xu 2022). Importantly, however, proponents of the latter view do not attribute any decline in inequality to redistributive efforts or wider structural changes to the Indian economy, but

rather to a slowdown of overall economic growth which, given India's unequal and labour-surplus economy, hits the wealthiest the most.
4 The hallmark of this commitment was arguably the introduction of the Special Economic Zones Act in 2005 which provided a legal framework for building hyperliberalised economic enclaves (Levien 2018; Nielsen 2018).
5 There is an extensive and well-established scholarship on the history, character and contemporary relevance of Hindu nationalism, the outline of which is beyond the scope of this book. Readers seeking accessible inroads into this literature may consult seminal work such as Jaffrelot (2007) and Hansen (1999).
6 Other scholars have likened this "aggressive corporatised economy" to a form of "roll-over neoliberalism" (Nielsen and Nilsen 2022b) where neoliberal reforms are promoted through authoritarian-populist means, more by force of unilateral action than through democratic consent, and where popular dissent is heavily and sometimes brutally policed. Others again invoke concepts such as "expedited neoliberalism" (Desai 2016) that bear promises of quick returns on investments, business-friendly policies, and overall pro-capital economic measures, to the benefit of dominant class interests. Among the many initiatives where this is visible, Modi's flagship "Make in India" programme (Chacko 2018) with its emphasis on ease of doing business indicators and FDI inflows is probably the most well-known.

References

Adaman, F., and Akbulut, B. 2021. Erdoğan's Three-pillared Neoliberalism: Authoritarianism, Populism and Developmentalism. *Geoforum 124:* 279–289.
Adcock, C., and Govindrajan, R. 2019. Bovine Politics in South Asia: Rethinking Religion, Law and Ethics. South Asia: Journal of South Asian Studies 42 (6): 1095–1107.
Ahmed, W., and Chatterjee, I. 2016. Antinomies of the Indian State. In *The Palgrave Handbook of Critical International Political Economy*, edited by Cafruny, A., Talani, L. S. and Martin, G. P., 331–349. London: Palgrave Macmillan.
Akram-Lodhi, H. 2022. I Will Follow? Authoritarian Populism, Past and Present. *Journal of Peasant Studies* 49 (6): 1316–1330.
Alavi, F. 2020. Explained: Here's How Uttar Pradesh Can Lead India in Buffalo Meat Exports. *CNBCTV*, 20 December, https://www.cnbctv18.com/india/explained-hereshow-uttar-pradesh-can-lead-india-in-buffalo-meat-exports-7836961.htm
Al Jazeera. 2022. India Slips in Global Hunger Index, Ranks 107 Out of 121 Nations. 15 October, https://www.aljazeera.com/news/2022/10/15/india-hunger
Anwar, T. 2018. Latehar Lynchings: A Saga of Cover-up, Political Connections and Police Negligence. *News Click,* 25 July, https://www.newsclick.in/latehar-lynching-saga-cover-political-connections-and-police-negligence
Banaji, J. 2022. Indian Big Business: The Evolution of India's Corporate Sector From 2000 to 2020. *Phenomenal World,* 20 December, https://www.phenomenalworld.org/analysis/family-business/
Bello, W. 2019. *Counterrevolution: The Global Rise of the Far Right.* Warwickshire: Practical Action Publishing.
Berberoglu, B. (ed.). 2020. *The Global Rise of Authoritarianism in the 21st Century: Crisis of Neoliberal Globalization and the Nationalist Response.* London: Routledge.
Bernstein, H. 2020. Unpacking "Authoritarian Populism" and Rural Politics: Some Comments on ERPI. Journal of Peasant Studies 47 (7): 1526–1542.

Bonefeld, W. 1992. Social Constitution and the Form of the Capitalist State. *Open Marxism* 1: 93–132.

Borras, S. M. 2020. Agrarian Social Movements: The Absurdly Difficult but Not Impossible Agenda of Defeating Right-wing Populism and Exploring a Socialist Future. *Journal of Agrarian Change* 20 (1): 3–36.

Chacko, P. 2018. The Right Turn in India: Authoritarianism, Populism and Neoliberalisation. Journal of Contemporary Asia 48 (4): 541–565.

Chancel, L., and Piketty, T. 2019. Indian Income Inequality, 1922–2015: From British Raj to Billionaire Raj? *Review of Income and Wealth* 65 (S1): S33–S62.

Chandra, R. 2020. Taking the Temperature of Capital. *Seminar* 734, https://www.indiaseminar.com/2020/734/734_rohit_chandra.htm

Chandra, R., and Verma, R. 2020. The Problem. *Seminar* 734, https://www.indiaseminar.com/2020/734/734_the_problem.htm

Chatterjee, E. 2023. India's Oligarchic State Capitalism. *Current History* 122 (843): 123–130.

Chatterjee, P. 2008. Democracy and Economic Transformation in India. *Economic and Political Weekly* 43 (16): 53–62.

Chatterji, A. P., Hansen, T. B., and Jaffrelot, C. (eds). 2019. *Majoritarian State: How Hindu Nationalism is Changing India*. Oxford: Oxford University Press.

Clarke, S. 1991. Chapter 1: The State Debate. In *The State Debate*, edited by Clarke, S., 1–69. London: Palgrave Macmillan.

Corbridge, S., and Harriss, J. 2000. *Reinventing India: Liberalization, Hindu Nationalism and Popular Democracy*. Cambridge: Policy Press.

Damodaran, H. 2020. From "Entrepeneurial" to "Conglomerate" Capitalism. *Seminar* 734, https://www.india-seminar.com/2020/734/734_harish_damodaran.htm

Desai, R. 2016. The Slow-Motion Counterrevolution: Developmental Contradictions and the Emergence of Neoliberalism. In *Social Movements and the State in India: Deepening Democracy?* edited by Nielsen, K. B. and Nilsen, A. G., 25–51. London: Palgrave Macmillan.

Dhara, T. 2017. India's Biggest Buff Meat Exporter Gets Govt Award for "Outstanding Performance". *News18,* 14 June, https://www.news18.com/news/india/indias-biggest-buff-meat-exporter-gets-govt-award-for-outstanding-performance-1432427.html

Dhingra, S. 2022. Why Coastal Karnataka is Southern India's "Hindutva Laboratory". *AlJazeera,* 5 August, https://www.aljazeera.com/news/2022/8/5/why-coastal-karnataka-is-southern-indias-hindutva-laboratory

Drèze, J., and Sen, A. 2013. *An Uncertain Glory: India and its Contradictions*. Princeton: Princeton University Press.

Echeverri-Gent, J., Sinha, A., and Wyatt, A. 2021. Economic Distress amidst Political Success: India's Economic Policy under Modi, 2014–2019. *India Review* 20 (4): 402–435.

Fischer, J. 2023. *Vegetarianism, Meat and Modernity in India*. London: Routledge.

Ghatak, M., Raghavan, R., and Xu, L. 2022. Trends in Economic Inequality in India. *The India Forum,* 19 September, https://www.theindiaforum.in/economy/trends-economic-inequality-india

Gopalakrishnan, S. 2006. Defining, Constructing and Policing a "New India": Relationship Between Neoliberalism and Hindutva. *Economic and Political Weekly* 41 (26): 2803–2813.

Gopalakrishnan, S. 2009. *Neoliberalism and Hindutva: Fascism, Free Markets, and the Restructuring of Indian Capitalism*. Delhi: Aakar Books.

Govindrajan, R. 2018. *Animal Intimacies: Interspecies Relatedness in India's Central Himalayas*. Chicago: Chicago University Press.

Gramsci, A. 1971. *Selections from the Prison Notebooks*. New York: International Publishers.

Gupta, A., and Sivaramakrishnan, K. 2011. Introduction: The State in India after Liberalization. In The State in India After Liberalization, edited by Gupta, A. and Sivaramakrishnan, K., 17 – 44. London: Routledge.

Hall, S. 2011. The Neo-Liberal Revolution. *Cultural Studies* 25 (6): 705–728.

Hansen, T. B. 1999. *The Saffron Wave: Democracy and Hindu Nationalism in Modern India*. Princeton: Princeton University Press.

Hansen, T. B. 2001. *Wages of Violence: Naming and Identity in Postcolonial Bombay*. Pricenton: Princeton University Press.

Hansen, T. B., and Roy, S. (eds). 2022. *Saffron Republic: Hindu Nationalism and State Power in India*. Cambridge: Cambridge University Press.

Hasan, Z. 2012. *Congress after Indira: Policy, Power, Political Change (1984–2009)*. Oxford: Oxford University Press.

Holloway, J., and Picciotto, S. 1978. Introduction: Towards a Materialist Theory of the State. In *The State and Capital: A Marxist Debate*, edited by Holloway, J. and Picciotto, S., 1–31. London: Edward Arnold.

HRW. 2019. Violent Cow Protection in India: Vigilante Groups Attack Minorities. *HRW*, 18 February, https://www.hrw.org/report/2019/02/19/violent-cow-protection-india/vigilante-groups-attack-minorities

Jaffrelot, C. (ed.). 2007. *Hindu Nationalism: A Reader*. Princeton: Princeton University Press.

Jaffrelot, C. 2015. The Class Element in the 2014 Indian Election and the BJP's Success with Special Reference to the Hindu Belt. *Studies in Indian Politics* 3 (1): 19–38.

Jaffrelot, C. 2019. Class and Caste in the 2019 Indian Election: Why Have So Many Poor Started Voting for Modi? *Studies in Indian Politics* 7 (2): 149–160.

Jaffrelot, C. 2021. *Modi's India: Hindu Nationalism and the Rise of Ethnic Democracy*. Princeton: Princeton University Press.

Jenkins, R. 1999. *Democratic Politics and Economic Reform in India*. Cambridge: Cambridge University Press.

Juego, B. 2017. The Philippines 2017: Duterte-led Authoritarian Populism and its Liberal-Democratic Roots. *Asia Maior* 129–163.

Kaur, R. 2020. *Brand New Nation: Capitalist Dreams and Nationalist Designs in Twenty-First-Century India*. Stanford: Stanford University Press.

Kellner, D. 2016. *American Nightmare: Donald Trump, Media Spectacle, and Authoritarian Populism*. Rotterdam: Sense Publishers.

Kothakapa, G., and Sirohi, R. A. 2023. "Capital as Power": An Alternative Reading of India's Post-2011 Economic Slowdown. *Area Development and Policy* 8 (1): 37–59.

Kumbamu, A. 2020. Saffron Fascism: The Conflux of Hindutva Ultra-Nationalism, Neoliberal Extractivism, and the Rise of Authoritarian Populism in Modi's India. In *The Global Rise of Authoritarianism in the 21st Century: Crisis of Neoliberal Globalization and the Nationalist Response*, edited by Berberoglu, B., 161–177. London: Routledge.

Levien, M. 2018. *Dispossession Without Development: Land Grabs in Neoliberal India*. Oxford: Oxford University Press.

Lührmann, A., et al. 2018. *Democracy for All? V-Dem Annual Democracy Report 2018*. Gothenburg: University of Gothenburg.

Mahapatra, R. 2012. Rise of Livestock. *Down to Earth*, 31 January, https://www.downtoearth.org.in/coverage/rise-of-livestock-35670

Mau, S. 2023. *Mute Compulsion: A Marxist Theory of the Economic Power of Capital*. London: Verso.

McKay, B. M., Oliveira, G. de L. T., and Liu, J. 2020. Authoritarianism, Populism, Nationalism and Resistance in the Agrarian South. Canadian Journal of Development Studies/Revue Canadienne d'études du Développement 41 (3): 347–362.

Muraleedharan, S. 2023. Narendra Modi's "Gujarat Model": Re-moulding Development in the Service of Religious Nationalism. *Commonwealth & Comparative Politics* 61 (29): 129–151.

Narayan, B. 2009. *Fascinating Hindutva: Saffron Politics and Dalit Mobilisation*. Delhi: Sage.

Narayanan, Y. 2023. *Mother Cow, Mother India: A Multispecies Politics of Dairy in India*. Stanford: Stanford University Press.

Nielsen, K. B. 2018. *Land Dispossession and Everyday Politics in Rural Eastern India*. London: Anthem Press.

Nielsen, K. B., and Nilsen, A. G. 2021. Love Jihad and the Governance of Gender and Intimacy in Hindu Nationalist Statecraft. *Religions* 12: 1068.

Nielsen, K. B., and Nilsen, A. G. 2022a. Hindu Nationalist Statecraft and Modi's Authoritarian Populism. In *Routledge Handbook on Autocratization in South Asia*, edited by Widmalm, S., 92–100. London: Routledge.

Nielsen, K. B., and Nilsen, A. G. 2022b. India's Evolving Neoliberal Regime of Dispossession: From the Anti-SEZ Movement to the Farm Law Protests. *Sociological Bulletin* 71 (4): 582–600.

Nielsen, K. B., Selvaraj, S., and Nilsen, A. G. Forthcoming. Hindu Nationalist Statecraft, Dog-whistle Legislation, and the Vigilante State in Contemporary India. *Swedish Journal of Anthropology* 6 (2).

Nilsen, A. G. 2021. India's Trajectories of Change, 2004–2019. In *Destroying Democracy: Neoliberal Capitalism and the Rise of Authoritarian Politics*, edited by Williams, M. and Satgar, V., 112–126. Johannesburg: Wits University Press.

Nilsen, A. G. 2023. Feast, Famine, and Hegemony: On Neoliberalisation and Hindu Nationalism in India. *Polity*, https://ssalanka.org/feast-famine-and-hegemony-on-neoliberalisation-and-hindu-nationalism-in-india-alf-gunvald-nilsen/

Oxfam India. 2022. *Inequality Kills – India Supplement 2022*. New Delhi: Oxfam India.

Palshikar, S. 2019. Toward Hegemony: The BJP Beyond Electoral Dominance. In *Majoritarian State: How Hindu Nationalism Is Changing India*, edited by Chatterji, A. P., Hansen, T. B. and Jaffrelot, C., 101–116. London: Hurst.

Patel, R. 2018. Islamophobia Gastronomica – On the Food Police, Rural Populism and Killing. *Open Democracy*, 26 February, https://www.opendemocracy.net/openIndia/raj-patel/islamophobia-gastronomica-on-food-police-rural-populism-and-killing

Pattenden, J. 2023. Progressive Politics and Populism: Classes of Labour and Rural–Urban Political Sociology – An Introduction to the Special Issue. *Journal of Agrarian Change* 23 (1): 3–21.

Peck, J., and Tickell, A. 2002. Neoliberalizing Space. *Antipode* 34 (3): 380–404.

Poulantzas, N. 1978. *State, Power, Socialism*. London: New Left Review Editions.
Poulantzas, N. 2008. *The Poulantzas Reader: Marxism, Law, and the State*. Edited by Martin, J. London: Verso.
Rajhansa, N., and Mukherjea, S. 2023. India's 20 Largest Profit Generators are Earning 80% of the Nation's Profits. The Wire, 12 January, https://thewire.in/economy/winner-takes-all-in-indias-new-improved-economy
Ramakrishnan, V. 2020. Uttar Pradesh: Hindutva Laboratory 2.0. *Frontline*, 18 October, https://frontline.thehindu.com/cover-story/hindutva-laboratory-20/article32882949.ece
Ruparelia, S. 2013. India's New Rights Agenda: Genesis, Promises, Risks. *Pacific Affairs* 86 (3): 569–590.
Ruud, A. 2023. Strongman: The Extraordinary Leaders of India and the Philippines. *Studies in Indian Politics* 11 (1): 27–38.
Scoones, I., Edelman, M., Borras, S. M., Hall, R., Wolford, W., and White, B. 2018. Emancipatory Rural Politics: Confronting Authoritarian Populism. Journal of Peasant Studies 45 (1): 1–20.
Sinha, S. 2021. "Strong Leaders", Authoritarian Populism and Indian Developmentalism: The Modi Moment in Historical Context. *Geoforum* 124: 320–333.
Sircar, N. 2020. The Politics of Vishwas: Political Mobilization in the 2019 National Election. *Contemporary South Asia* 28 (2): 178–194.
Sircar, N. 2022. Corporate-controlled Capitalism in India. *Seminar* 749, https://www.india-seminar.com/2022/749/749-NEELANJAN%20SIRCAR.htm
Staples, J. 2020. *Sacred Cows and Chicken Manchurian: The Everyday Politics of Eating Meat in India*. Seattle: University of Washington Press.
Subramaniam, T., and Farooqui, S. 2023. Too Few Jobs, Too Many Workers and no "Plan B": The Time Bomb Hidden in India's "Economic Miracle". *CNN*, 27 May, https://edition.cnn.com/2023/05/27/economy/india-economic-miracle-issues-youth-intl-hnk-dst/index.html
Sud, N. 2022. The Actual Gujarat Model: Authoritarianism, Capitalism, Hindu Nationalism and Populism in the Time of Modi. *Journal of Contemporary Asia* 52 (1): 102–126.
Tamaki, E. R., Mendonça, R. F., and Ferreira, M. G. M. 2021. The Symbolic Construction of a Messiah: Jair Bolsonaro's Public, Christian Discourse. In *When Politicians Talk: The Cultural Dynamics of Public Speaking*, edited by Feldman, O., 73–89. Singapore: Springer.
Widmalm, S. (ed.). 2021. *Routledge Handbook of Autocratization in South Asia*. London: Routledge.
Wood, E. M. 1995. *Democracy against Capitalism: Rewriting Historical Materialism*. Cambridge: Cambridge University Press.

2 Hindu Nationalism and Bovine Political Economy

In an interview with *India Times* in 2017, the self-proclaimed cow protectionist, or *gau rakshak*, Manjeet Arya, spoke about what motivated him and his fellow cow protectionists: "For us, anybody who harms a cow is a villain irrespective of caste, creed and religion … How can one eat a cow?", Arya asked rhetorically. The cow is pious in Hinduism, he continued, and should not be seen as a food: "I don't know about other countries, but in India where the majority sees the cow as the mother, it should be protected and will be at every cost", he concluded (Arya cited in *India Times* 2017).

India Times' feature article carrying the interview with Arya is just one among very many indicators of how bovine politics and cow protectionism have become central to contemporary Hindu nationalism. This has happened in two distinct yet interrelated ways. In the legal domain, bovines are protected by increasingly strict legislation across most of India's states; while in the extra-legal domain, vigilante groups take it upon themselves to protect the cow "at every cost", ready to inflict violence on people who harm the cow.

This Hindu nationalist "political moment" of Modi's authoritarian populism, however, needs to be analysed along with its "economic" counterpart to which it is inextricably related. This chapter seeks to do this. Separating the political and the economic for purely heuristic purposes, we start by attending to the political moment, proceeding from a brief discussion of the "bovine symbolism" (Staples 2020: 12) of Hindu nationalist politics to an analysis of legal and extra-legal forms of cow protectionism that have mushroomed during Modi's years in power. We show how cow veneration, legal protectionism, and street vigilantism work together to draw boundaries between "true Indians" and their anti-national enemies. In doing so, they advance the larger hegemonic project of the BJP and allied Hindu nationalist organisations of turning India into a Hindu state, through violent xenophobia and racism of the kind that defines authoritarian populism more generally (Borras 2020). We subsequently turn to the economic "moment" as we analyse class dynamics and patterns of capital accumulation in the bovine economy, focusing particularly on the relations between Modi's state, his authoritarian populism, and those fractions of capital that seek to further corporate growth in the bovine meat sector. Our analysis of the socio-political Hindutva "moment" of Modi's authoritarian populism and its intertwined neoliberalising economic "moment" brings to light a significant state contradiction at the heart of Modi's India, whose unfolding in the realm of the country's bovine political economy is further explored in subsequent chapters.

Bovine Symbolism and the Meaning of Bovines

As James Staples (2020: 11) has argued, any attempt to discover the definitive meaning of bovine animals and their products within the Indian context is, even at a single point in history, doomed to failure. This is the case not only because of India's great social and cultural diversity, but also because of the multiple, co-existing, partly overlapping and partly contradictory regimes of classification that govern bovine bodies. As Narayanan (2018) has shown, even Hindutva activists and vigilantes who rally around the seemingly universal demand for cow protectionism and a ban on the slaughter of cows may at the same time distinguish and discriminate between three categories of bovines: The native Indian-bred cow; the crossbreeds or foreign species such as Jersey and Holstein-Friesian bovines; and the buffalo. This division is, in a caste-like manner, highly stratified. Only the native or "desi" breeds are regarded as "pure" (akin to a Brahman) and considered worthy of protection and veneration. The crossbreeds are regarded as a socially inferior mixed breed, or a "low-caste monstrosity" (ibid.: 344). Conceived of as lazy, highly prone to disease, and incapable of displaying emotions, the crossbreeds are by some Hindu nationalists not even regarded as a cow at all (Narayanan 2023: 152, 184). The buffalo ranks even lower, as a "demonic", ritually devalued and innately contemptible animal explicitly referenced as low caste (Narayanan 2018: 346). Only the "virtuous" domestic breeds are deemed capable of supplying the five sacred products of milk, butter, ghee, urine, and dung that are used in Hindu ritual purification; only its milk is seen as "pure", while that of the Jersey and Holstein-Friesian cows are deemed "corrupting" or "spiritually base", causing harmful ideas in people's minds and leading them into criminality (Narayanan 2023: 168; Staples 2020: 31).

For those who *consume* bovine meat, however, the distinctions between different kinds of bovines and different kinds of bovine meat may be considerably more blurred to the point of being irrelevant. As Staples (2020: 31–33, 92) observed from South India, butchers simply tended to sell the meat of whatever animal they could source most easily and at the most competitive rates on a given day, with little regard for what kind of animal the meat came from. Among those who purchased and consumed beef, Muslims would often have a clear preference for cow beef, while Dalit Hindus and some Christians tended to favour buffalo meat. But rarely would customers question the butcher about the provenance of the animal, and most people would simply treat meat from a buffalo and meat from a cow as one and the same thing.

Farmers and other owners of cattle also discriminate between different types of bovines in complex ways that sometimes align with, but often depart from those hierarchically stratified categorisations that Hindu nationalists operate with. In her work in rural Uttarakhand, Govindrajan (2018) found that local villagers did indeed distinguish between Jersey cows and indigenous *katu* or *pahari* cows. The two were different in body and behaviour. Because of the Jersey's strong connection to dairying and its plentiful milk, it was spoken of as a "business cow" or a "modern cow", a "cow with style". Yet its milk was thinner and less strongly flavoured, its urine and dung watery with less nutritional and health benefits, and its body ritually feeble and weak. These were, in contrast, qualities that the native cow and its products had, along with moral and physical strength and genuine *shakti* or divine power, which the Jerseys entirely lacked. While these differences, and particularly the *shakti* and ritual efficacy of the *pahari* cow, may eventually make the Jersey more killable than the *pahari* cow, it did not make her unlovable in the way that Hindu vigilantes may have imagined (Govindrajan 2018: 81). And, importantly, the distinction between the two did not emerge from within a Hindu nationalist framework that saw "foreign species" as inherently threatening to the identity and strength of the Hindu nation. Rather, it emerged from an embodied, intimate knowledge of the nature of bovine bodies and behaviour, derived from people's everyday quotidian immersion in their cows' lives, which made them recognise that these animals were materially different. Govindrajan's analysis is thus also a timely reminder of how bovine bodies cannot be reduced to mere passive receptables of symbolic meaning but are rather lively and unpredictable in ways that make their meaning particularly difficult to fix and contain (Govindrajan 2018: 71–72). Comparably, Kathryn Hardy's (2019) study of dairy-keeping backward caste Yadavs in north India found that among this community, it is the buffalo – and not the cow – that has ritual importance, thereby undermining the claim that buffalos can only symbolise the demonic.

Irrespective of the configuration of distinctions between different species, other distinctions are also significant for owners of cows and cattle, particularly the economic one between "productive" and "unproductive" animals. While the former contribute to the wealth and wellbeing of the household, the latter will be considered a drain on scarce resources and are likely to eventually be sold off, even if this may happen with considerable emotional costs. Legal regimes that protect bovines to various degrees may operate with yet other distinctions. Cow protection legislation does generally not distinguish between native and foreign species but regulates or prohibits the slaughter of cows irrespective of species. Often, they distinguish between cows and buffaloes, but not always. Rather, the age of the cattle may be a legal criterion, such as when one or more species of cattle over a certain age are permitted for slaughter while younger animals are not.

While the existence of such multiple, partly overlapping, partly contradictory classificatory regimes arguably creates fertile conditions of possibility for many forms of bovine politics, the bovine politics that we analyse in this chapter is driven primarily by the instrumentalised use of bovine bodies real or imagined in a violent project of Hindu majoritarianism, fuelled by suspicion, rumour, and gossip. As such, bovine bodies emerge as central sites for the Hindu nationalist project of turning India into a Hindu state – a key aspect of Modi's authoritarian populism.

Cow Protectionism and Its Discontents

Hindu nationalists and fundamentalists uphold cow-veneration and vegetarianism as millennia-old cultural traditions that define Hinduism as a religious practice.[1] In contrast, secular historians have shown that the elevation of the cow to sacred status for *all* Hindus is a more recently invented and historically contested tradition. A widely referenced case in point is historian D. N. Jha's (2002) book *The Myth of the Holy Cow*. Published in 2002, the book is arguably the most well-known effort at exploding the long-held myth of an unbroken history of Hindu cow reverence and vegetarianism. In this book, Jha outlines substantial textual evidence of ritual killing, eating, and sacrifice of allegedly "holy" cows throughout Hindu history, showing how cow meat was part of early Indian non-vegetarian dietary traditions. In India, the book caused controversy even before it was published. As excerpts were posted on the Internet and picked up by newspapers, the book was cancelled by the publisher, burned by religious activists, and called "sheer blasphemy" by a spokesman for the Hindu nationalist World Hindu Council (VHP). Jha also received death threats (Eakin 2002).

The history of cow protectionism as a political tactic is of a relatively recent date and can be traced back to the latter half of the 19th century when it was deployed to assert Hindu identity and unify diverse castes and communities (Freitag 1980). In the colonial context, the cow was an eminently useful symbol for highlighting and politicising the perceived differences between Muslims (who ate it) and Hindus (who revered it), and for moving this difference into the domain of public agitation. During the 1880s, cow protection societies, or *gaurakshini sabhas*, were formed and were particularly active in North India. These societies petitioned the colonial government and fought legal battles in the name of the cow, but also organised processions that led to deadly communal clashes between Hindus and Muslims (Metcalf and Metcalf 1998: 150–155). Among Hindu nationalists, this "rallying round the cow" (Pandey 1981) was to produce a shared sense of Hindu identity and unity, with India's Muslim minority cast as the antagonistic "other". It was through the cow that community, nation, and religion were conjoined, and by referring to the cow as "mother", Hindu nationalists sought to evoke the same imagery as the term "Mother India": Symbolic purity and virtue that must be protected at all costs from those who threaten the Hindu nation (Gittinger 2017; Narayanan 2023).

Although *The Myth of the Holy Cow* is first and foremost a historical study, Jha also observed – with what in hindsight appears as a certain understatement – how the killing of cattle had "emerged again and again as a troublesome issue on the Indian political scene even in independent India" (Jha 2002: 19). Indeed, just five years after India had become an independent nation, the Hindu nationalist organisation the Rashtriya Swayamsevak Sangh (RSS) – of which Modi is a lifelong member – collected upwards of 17 million signatures on a petition that demanded a national ban on cow slaughter. The RSS had been banned in early 1948, because of suspicion of its involvement in the murder of Mahatma Gandhi, whose assassin was a former member of the RSS. The ban was lifted in July 1949 (Andersen and Damle 2019: xii), and the petition against cow slaughter was the RSS's first mass public agitation after independence. Cow protection and a national ban on cow slaughter have remained a core issue with the RSS ever since. In the mid-1960s, for example, the RSS spearheaded a "great all-party campaign" for the protection of the cow that eventually attempted to storm the Indian parliament to pressure legislators to criminalise cow slaughter in the entire country (Copland 2014). The forerunner of the BJP, the Bharatiya Jan Sangh, similarly made cow protection one of its core elements from the early 1950s. While the politicisation of cow protectionism has thus largely been associated with the Hindu right, it has also been widely endorsed by the self-professed secular Congress party, and many Congress-ruled states have over time passed laws restricting or banning the slaughter of cattle.

In the decade leading up to the publication of Jha's book, cow protection had gradually become less important within the RSS and BJP as priorities shifted towards economic growth and liberalisation under the Vajpayee government. However, it remained a core issue with other organisations within the larger Hindu nationalist movement, and in recent years it has assumed an unprecedented centrality to Indian political discourse. It has even acquired a certain positive global resonance. Globally, the stereotypical, even caricature image of India as an overwhelmingly vegetarian country populated by cow-worshipping, otherworldly Hindus who practice non-violence towards all living creatures is a well-established one, and cow veneration and vegetarianism are widely seen as benign aspects of India's cultural heritage. At the current conjuncture where the accelerating meatification of global diets is a cause for grave environmental concern, and where large-scale environmental destruction calls for more sustainable ways of living, veneration for non-human sentient beings coupled with vegetarianism can be said to constitute important components in India's soft power arsenal, alongside postcolonial democracy, yoga, and Bollywood. Within India, however, the resurgence of cow protectionism since 2014 when Modi came to power has been far from "soft", to the extent that the issue has consolidated as one of the most polarising tools of political segregation between Hindus and Muslims (Vij 2016). As we show below, on the one hand – and as part of a broader pattern of writing Hindu nationalism into law (Nielsen and Nilsen 2021, 2022) – ever-stricter laws have been passed to "protect the cow"; on the other hand, vigilante groups are increasingly policing and punishing those who do not sufficiently respect the cow.

Cow Protection through Law

Cow protection is under article 48 of the Indian Constitution a "state subject", meaning that there is no central law on this question that applies to the whole country. Rather, India has "a patchwork of state laws on cow protection, ranging from no bans to total prohibition" (Andersen and Damle 2019: 177). While a systematic review of this "patchwork" is beyond the scope of this book, we note that some form of cow protection now exists in a large majority of India's states and Union Territories.[2] Three quarters of the states banning cow slaughter make it a cognisable offence, alongside crimes such as rape, murder, and theft, while in half it is a non-bailable offence – alongside crimes such as sedition, counterfeiting, and trafficking. Modi is known to favour a national ban on cow slaughter (ibid.: 179), and while such a national ban has so far not materialised, state-level legislative changes have systematically made the slaughter of cows (or even the sale and possession of cow beef) illegal in ever-larger parts of the country under Modi (Jaffrelot 2019: 59).[3]

Modi's home state of Gujarat, for instance, in 2017 amended an act from 1954 that criminalised cow slaughter, the transportation of cows for slaughter, and the possession of beef, to extend the maximum sentence for cow slaughter to life imprisonment. Other BJP-controlled states such as Maharashtra and Haryana have also toughened cow protection legislation by criminalising beef consumption in 2015. The former imposed a total ban on the slaughter of all cattle (bulls and bullocks included) and completely banned all transport of cattle out of the state (Ramdas 2017a). It also initially criminalised the mere possession of cow meat, although this clause was later decriminalised by the High Court, provided that the animal from which the meat came had been slaughtered outside of Maharashtra. Maharashtra in addition appointed honorary animal welfare officers to implement the new law. Among those appointed as officers were a number of former cow protection activists (Jaffrelot 2021: 220). In Haryana – the state with the most vigorous cow protection operations (Jaffrelot 2021: 220) – the slaughter of cows was criminalised with jail sentences of up to ten years and heavy fines. To implement the law, the state police set up a so-called "cow task force" (Jaffrelot 2019: 62). In 2019, the Haryana law was further tightened when an amendment was introduced, allowing police officers to enter, stop, and search any vehicle used or intended to be used for the sale of cows or beef; to seize cows or beef along with transportation vehicles; and to enter and search any premises used or intended to be used for the slaughter of cows (*Business Standard* 2019).

Uttar Pradesh has similarly introduced unprecedentedly strict legal punishments for various offences ranging from cow slaughter to "endangering the life of cows" by, for example, not providing them food and water. This has occurred under the leadership of the hardliner Hindu nationalist chief minister Yogi Adityanath who has a long history of engagement in cow protectionism predating his time as Chief Minister. In 1998 when Adityanath was first elected to the Lok Sabha, he established the Gau Raksha Manch (cow protection front), an organisation that recruited and trained young Hindus according to the tenets of Hindu nationalism (Jaffrelot 2021: 222–225). Adityanath's cow protection front was later converted into a militia named the Hindu Yuva Vahini, the Hindu youth brigade, described by the journalist Dhirendra K. Jha (2017: 43, 54) as "a squad of goons" with "testosterone-fuelled unemployed young men running amok as cadres". The violent enforcement of the protection of cows remains high on the agenda of the Hindu Yuva Vahini, along with the targeting of "the meat-eating 'habits' of Muslims" (Jha 2017: 38). Uttar Pradesh is also among those states – along with, for example, Gujarat and Rajasthan – that have introduced legal amendments enabling the confiscation of vehicles alleged to be transporting cattle for slaughter (Ramdas 2020). Comparable legal restrictions were put in place in the southern state of Karnataka. Under BJP rule, Karnataka in 2020 passed the Prevention of Slaughter and Preservation of Cattle Bill (2020) that not only banned the slaughter of all cows, bulls, bullocks, and calves, but also outlawed the slaughter of buffaloes below the age of 13, made smuggling and transporting animals for slaughter a criminal offense, and empowered the police to conduct searches based on suspicion (Daniyal 2020).[4] What we have seen under Modi is, in other words, a profusion of legislative instruments that protect the cow, and which penalise offenders with potentially long jail sentences and heavy fines.

Extra-Legal Cow Protection and Vigilantism

Enhanced legal protection for the cow has gone hand in hand with a steep rise in cow protection vigilantism as armed gangs of cow protectionists – so-called *gau rakshaks* – of predominantly young men affiliated with various Hindu nationalist organisations have taken it upon themselves to "protect the cow". Although their often spectacularly violent actions frequently make headlines, very little is in fact known about the socio-economic background of the vigilantes, or their very diverse motivations for joining these groups. As Narayanan's research on *gau rakshaks* shows, vigilantism is often heavily incentivised financially and many join for financial reasons as the vigilante groups are often sponsored by Hindu charitable organisations. These may pay the vigilantes a regular salary, sponsor their children's education, and sometimes even provide a pension plan for family members. In some states, governments also offer financial rewards for seized cows. Other vigilantes may be motivated by a genuine love and concern for animals, including but not limited to cows, while others yet are certainly motivated by self-righteous outrage against those who, in their view, violate and torment "the Hindu cow" (Narayanan 2023: 190–198). The vigilante groups typically roam the roads in search of culprits transporting cows for slaughter, or track down people claimed to have killed cows, ready to beat, maim, rape, or kill people, and Muslims, in particular. In many cases, they also violently humiliate their victims, for example, by force-feeding them cow dung to "purify" their souls. Their operations are often based on rumours about water buffalo traders and handlers illegally transporting cows for slaughter. Frequently tech-savvy, vigilante groups are known to utilise social media to broadcast their activities, including by livestreaming their so-called "raids" (Taskin 2023).

Such extra-legal cow protectionism is closely intertwined with the new legislative instruments protecting the cow that we analysed above. In Karnataka, for example, a section of the law criminalising the slaughter of cattle specified that "persons acting in good faith" to uphold this law shall not face legal persecution. As the BJP's Deputy Chief Minister of the state said in 2020, this clause was specifically formulated "keeping in mind cow vigilantes ... vigilantes or anyone who is working for a cause and the law of the land should definitely have a scope to work in this provision" (*Deccan Herald* 2020). In this sense, an important function of the stronger legal restrictions on cow slaughter, transportation, and consumption appears to be to enable and even encourage vigilante groups to act as law enforcers through extra-legal violence and with relative impunity (see also Adcock 2019).

The vigilante groups the Deputy Chief Minister was referring to are not part of the state apparatus, but form part of the new power structure under the BJP qua their ideological and sometimes organisational closeness to the party in power. This includes the Akhil Bharatiya Vidyarthi Parishad, the student wing of the RSS, which has been involved in violent attacks on university student associations over beef eating (Ilaiah Shepherd 2019). Another organisation frequently involved in vigilante acts is the Bajrang Dal, the youth wing of the RSS. Members of the Bhartiya Gau Raksha Dal – another RSS wing, in charge of the country's *gaushala* initiative, which we return to in chapter three – are also reported to be part of many vigilante acts. The close proximity these vigilante groups have to Modi's regime and the broader Hindu nationalist movement of which it is part is thus both evident and well documented, also in cases where vigilante groups are less overtly linked to the RSS yet nevertheless function as its "shadow armies" (Jha 2017; see also Jaffrelot 2021).

In a rare example of up-close reporting on cow vigilantism, a journalist from *The Guardian* (Safi 2016) travelled with a group of *gau rakshaks* north of Delhi in 2016, documenting some of the typical activities involved, such as the patrolling of highways and country roads at night, searching for cows being transported. The men, in their twenties and thirties, were armed with rifles and revolvers, patrolling in convoys of some three dozen vigilantes, travelling in four-wheelers. *The Guardian* described the vigilantes as "daily wage labourers" from the relatively unprivileged local strata – in our terms, classes of labour. This observation about the class background of *gau rakshaks* resonates with Narayanan's (2023: 190–198) findings in her work on cow vigilantism. Most of the young men engaged in the actual "labour of militant protectionism" were, Narayanan writes, relatively poor and financially dependent on the money that came from the Hindu organisations that sponsored their activities. For some vigilantes, this was in fact the first time in their life they had enjoyed any measure of financial security. The particular group of cow protectionists written about by *The Guardian* had seen five of their own members killed during "raids" so far, something which underscores the paradoxical fact that cow vigilantes often work at considerable risk to themselves. Involving frantic search for cows in transport vehicles along the highway, the night's patrol was "revelrous" and "driven by a mob energy", according to the observing journalist, with police officers watching passively while the *gau rakshaks* inspected vehicles for suspect content. While the night's patrol did not bring much more of a "catch" than a single cattle transport that turned out to have all its licenses in order and thus had to be allowed to go, the men told the reporter stories of other nights, much more violent and sometimes deadly (Safi 2016). Studies such as the one by *The Guardian* illustrate the complex modalities through which certain classes of labour are incorporated into Hindu nationalism's hegemonic project to form part of its social and electoral support base, combining financial incentives with the "wages of violence" associated with public vigilantism and the "psychological wages" that flow from inclusion into a broader, assertive and ascendant project of Hindu unity.

Muslim cattle transporters have become favourite targets for these self-appointed cow protectors, who often work in close conjunction with the police and a wider network of informers who forewarn vigilantes about expected trucks carrying cattle and the particularities of their route (Narayanan 2023: 241). In contrast, Hindu cattle and cattle transporters are generally spared (Jaffrelot 2019: 60), thus underlining the crucial role of anti-Muslim sentiments in contemporary cow vigilantism. Yet Dalits, the formerly untouchable castes, have also been targeted by such groups. In one much-publicised incident, seven Dalits were thrashed and urinated upon in Modi's home state of Gujarat for performing their traditional occupation, namely skinning cows (Manor 2019: 123). In early 2019, in a report that drew significant international attention, Human Rights Watch reported that 44 people had been killed since 2015 and 280 people injured in vigilante attacks against cattle traders across the country. Sadly, these numbers fall far short of capturing the full extent of the violence and atrocities of contemporary cow vigilantism. Nor do they capture how vigilante violence is conjoined with more insidious scientific technologies including "beef detection kits" and "water buffalo detection kits". While these are ostensibly designed to prevent vigilante attacks, they in effect multiply the ways bovine bodies are involved in the surveillance and disciplining of certain populations (Parikh and Miller 2019).[5]

Such violent "Islamophobic gastronomy" as a way of adjudicating over citizenship, pitting classes of labour against each other, is widespread in authoritarian populisms more generally (Patel 2018). Cow veneration, legal protectionism, and street vigilantism thus work together to draw boundaries between "true Indians" (Hindus who revere the cow) and their anti-national enemies within (Muslims who eat or slaughter it). In this way, cows and beef in combination play crucial roles within the larger political project of the BJP and allied Hindu nationalist organisations. In effect, they partake of a new formation of the state, the formation of a *de facto* and increasingly also *de jure* Hindu *rashtra* (Jaffrelot 2019: 65) through unofficial and often violent forms of social and moral regulation that unfold with tacit or overt endorsement by the state, and which are increasingly backed by law. It is far from an uncontested project, and it has been resisted from several quarters, most spectacularly through "beef festivals" organised in different parts of India, on campuses by university students, and in public spaces in cities by political parties, where Dalits, in particular, have used them to assert a counter-hegemonic identity in opposition to the deeply Brahmanical version of Hinduism promoted by Hindu nationalists (Fischer 2023: 120–132; Natrajan 2018). Tellingly, in states such as Andhra Pradesh and Kerala, beef festivals organised on campuses over the last decade have been met with violent opposition by the RSS student organisation Akhil Bharatiya Vidyarthi Parishad.

Despite such contestation and resistance, however, the political Hindutva "moment" remains on a strong footing. Nonetheless, as we discuss next, a decisive state contradiction arises in relation to the economic "moment" of neoliberalisation under which India has seen concerted efforts at boosting agricultural exports and spurring capital accumulation by integration with growing transnational markets. Here, India's beef meat industry plays a prominent role.

Bovine Economy: The Political Economy of India's Bovine Agro-Industry

The surge in violent attention to beef eating under Modi that we analysed above is paralleled in a contradictory way by a dramatic surge in beef exports. In 2015, Modi's second year in office, India emerged for the first time as the world's largest exporter of beef meat from buffaloes, and it has remained one of the top exporters since. Opening agrarian sectors for increased export orientation is part-and-parcel of the assertive neoliberal economic policies of the Modi government, and although the rapid growth in beef exports began under the earlier UPA government, they have stabilised at a high level under Modi, both in terms of value and quantity (see Figure 2.1).[6]

34 Hindu Nationalism and Bovine Political Economy

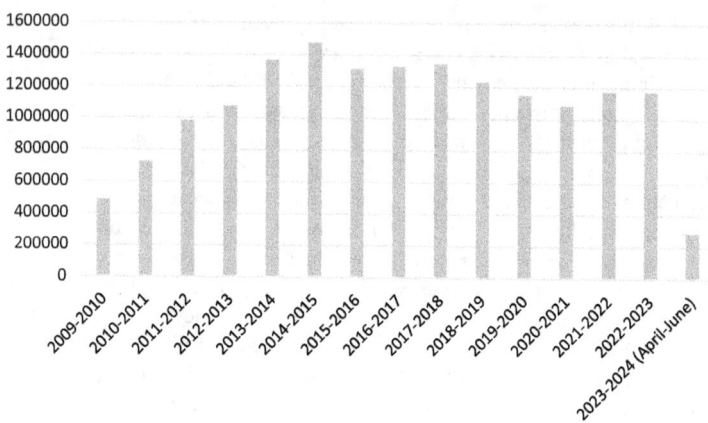

Figure 2.1 India's buffalo meat exports: Quantity in tonnes (MT).

Source: Compiled by authors based on data from the Agricultural and Processed Food Products Export Development Authority.

Despite its size, the Indian export sector cannot compete with advanced industrial livestock operations in other countries and has therefore specialised on "meeting demand in the fastest growing segment of the world beef market, primarily among low- and middle-income countries in Asia and the Middle East" (Landes et al. 2016). Vietnam was for long by far the largest market. Peaking at an export flow at 1.8 billion USD in 2018, it comprised the third largest single trade flow in meat globally.[7] India's exports to Vietnam at the time flowed further into China, one of the world's largest markets in meat (Jakobsen and Hansen 2020). Among other key markets for Indian beef are largely Muslim countries such as Malaysia, Egypt, Indonesia, Iraq, Saudi Arabia, and United Arab Emirates, but also a country such as the Philippines with only a small Muslim population (Press Information Bureau Delhi 2021).

Studies from the 1970s found that the dominant mechanism of eliminating cattle in India was starvation resulting in so-called natural death. The reasons cited at the time were "Hindu sentiments" and "the absence of a widespread and well-organised slaughter industry" (Nair 1981). Against this backdrop, the surge in beef exports from 2008 to 2014 is spectacular. The volume of Indian beef exports expanded by 17 percent annually (Landes et al. 2016), peaking at 1.475 million metric tonnes. This period saw sustained governmental efforts at strengthening the export industry, including India's National Meat and Poultry Processing Board, established in 2009. During the last decades, as we can surmise, buffalo meat production in India has increased significantly, with numbers from the UN's Food and Agriculture Organization showing a 54.1 percentage increase from 1990 to 2018.

To further unravel the state contradiction surrounding the bovine economy, we in the following pay attention to class dynamics and patterns of capital accumulation. To do so, we first explore the neoliberal restructuring of the bovine economy since the 1990s; and second, the relations between Modi's state, his authoritarian populism, and the fractions of capital pushing further corporate growth in the bovine meat sector.

The Restructuring of the Bovine Economy: Class and Accumulation Dynamics

Once we look more closely at the political economy of India's beef agro-industry, we can identify a progressive shift from a livestock economy based on decentralised, informal production among rural classes of labour, to an expanding export sector driving novel accumulation patterns based on corporate concentration and dominant class interests, facilitated (uneasily) by the Indian state. These recent developments towards growing meat exports through corporate concentration mark a politically strained consolidation of restructuring processes that have, in fact, been unfolding since the 1990s. We trace this process in detail below.

While the Hindu nationalist ideology of cow veneration and vegetarianism clearly implies "a gross misrepresentation of reality" as most of the Indian population, in fact, consumes meat (Natrajan and Jacob 2018: 63), India's overall meat consumption does remain very low compared to other middle-income countries where the "meatification" (Weis 2013) of diets has occurred with increasing pace. Globally, "the average human now consumes 43 kg of meat annually, almost a doubling since the 1960s" (Jakobsen and Hansen 2020). In contrast, India remains among the countries in the world that consume the least meat of any kind, with an overall consumption of 12 kg meat (of any kind) per capita in 2020 – including fish and seafood. The consumption of poultry has, however, grown considerably (Staples 2020: 119–139), and is more than double that of beef.[8] In this sense, poultry is the main area of meatification of Indian diets (Jakobsen 2020). Still, although data from household consumption surveys reveal an increase in meat consumption from the 2000s (Srinivas 2018), India's move towards anything approximating a "meat modernity" (Fischer 2023) has happened very slowly.

The main domestic function of the livestock economy is thus not to produce meat for domestic consumption. Rather, bovines are used for milk production and domestic milk consumption, with a "near doubling of aggregate milk consumption as food in India between the early 1980s and the late 1990s" (Khan and Bidabadi 2004: 107). This spectacular growth is, in turn, the result of what has been described as India's "White Revolution" in the dairy industry that has unfolded since the 1970s, with massive state support (Scholten 2010), making India the world's largest dairy nation. The livestock sector behind such massive milk production is estimated to comprise as much as 535.78 million animals, employing around 20 million people directly and many more indirectly along the value chain, and contributing to the livelihoods of around two-thirds of the rural population. In contrast to other leading beef producing and exporting countries, then, India does not rear bovines specifically for beef production. Rather, the Indian bovines whose meat is consumed at home or exported abroad are "discarded animals" from dairying. In this sense, "the milk-and-beef economy operate as a conjoined continuum" (Narayanan 2023: 184) where the beef industry is both an outcome of dairy farming as well as supportive of it by providing a solution to the dairy industry's problem of what to do with unproductive cattle (Govindrajan 2018: 65). To a considerable extent, beef can in fact be seen as a by-product of Indian dairy, and the large-scale slaughter and consumption of bovines as an inevitable outcome of a dairy industry that discards "useless", "spent", or "surplus" animals when they no longer serve the purpose of milk production – including males and non-milking females. As such, butchers, abattoirs, retail meat sellers, and global beef exporters, argues Narayanan (2023) persuasively, are as much a part of the milk production line as the dairy farmer and the milkman – and vice versa.

India's livestock economy is largely decentralised, and most livestock owners have only a single (or a few) buffalo or cow, reared, grazed and utilised within households rather than industrialised operations (Dorin and Landy 2009: 134). Official numbers hold that the average "herd size" for bovines is as little as two animals.[9] The most recent government report on livestock ownership shows that livestock-rearing is most commonly reported among households with "marginal" (73.14 percent) and "small" (13.74 percent) landholdings as well as landless households.[10] In our terms, vast proportions of the country's livestock are thus within the domain of classes of labour in the countryside. In a very similar way, the slaughter of bovines was until two or three decades ago largely an informal, small-scale affair. Numbers from the 1990s described abattoirs as overwhelmingly "small, unlicensed units", and identified only around 25 "relatively large" units sufficiently "geared to the export market" (Dorin and Landy 2009: 136). As we show below, the recent expansions of the export sector dominated by capitalist enterprises therefore entail novel accumulation patterns that differ markedly from how the livestock economy functions within the livelihoods of the country's classes of labour.

There are clear differences in the production systems involved in the export sector, and the domestic economy organised around classes of labour, respectively. Both domestic and export uses start with animals primarily reared by (very often non-beef eating) small and marginal farmers or landless labourers, who wish to sell their animals, especially culled dairy animals (FICCI 2013; Landes et al. 2016).[11] One option is for farmers to sell directly to a butcher, with the formal or informal aid of a broker. The second, and perhaps more common option is to sell to a livestock market, fair or auction, also with the intervention of a broker. From this point, however, the two systems depart. Those who supply the domestic market will transport cattle purchased from markets or fairs to the municipal slaughterhouses, where the animal is slaughtered, and the meat subsequently sold fresh from small sales outlets to the last link in the chain, the individual, domestic purchaser and consumer of meat (Staples 2020: 81–92). The export chains, in contrast, have traders selling to other actors, namely export-oriented operations running more integrated processing facilities that then supply export firms (Ramdas 2017b). The latter enterprises need to be registered with the Agricultural and Processed Food Products Export Development Authority and comply with associated routines and procedures for assessing and checking facilities and products, thus departing fully from the informal livestock system described above. This reveals a break, we would emphasise, in terms of class and accumulation patterns in the political economy of India's bovine agro-industry.

Writing in 2013, Zarin Ahmad (2013) observed that the structure of the meat industry was changing rapidly, altering the organisational structure, ownership, technologies, and supply chain of the meat industry, leading to the emergence of a few relatively large firms owning the entire chain of production. In this context, the large export firms and associated meat processors emerge as key new actors in what is thus a highly concentrated industry with a limited number of players. An industry source from 2017 speaks of around 150 Indian beef exporters, with the top ten companies representing a mix of ownership interests, seemingly including also Muslim-owned, halal-industry oriented exporters (Export Genious 2017).[12] As a quick casual Google search will reveal, this latter factor has led to numerous recent online claims pushed by Hindu nationalist "trolls" to the effect that beef export is a Muslim phenomenon.[13] This has, in turn, been met by counterclaims pointing to the main dominance of upper-caste Hindu business elites over key firms in the sector. This controversy notwithstanding, it is clear that the sector is highly concentrated. Some sources mention a mere 49 registered slaughter/processing facilities for export (Landes et al. 2016), others as little as 13 completely export-oriented processing units.[14] Moreover, companies located in just a few states dominate the industry – Uttar Pradesh as the most prominent, followed by Maharashtra, Andhra Pradesh, and Punjab.[15] This clustering by states may in fact gloss over an even more intense form of clustering as the main meat export firms are concentrated in a few cities alone, with Mumbai and New Delhi accounting for 66 percent of the revenue in the industry, according to one source (Export Genius 2017). Concentration ostensibly also appears in ownership, leading one commentator to hold that India's meat export industry is "owned by just a clutch of people" (Anand 2014).

While reliable facts about the industry are hard to find, the Mumbai-based Allanasons Pvt Ltd is considered the leading company. As our opening vignettes to the book brought out, in the years 2014–2015 and 2015–2016, the company exported buffalo meat worth around INR 10,000 crore each year. With total beef exports standing at around INR 25,700 crore, this means that Allanasons exported more than a third of India's buffalo meat (Chakraborty 2017). A report on beef exports during the first quarter of 2017 supports this estimate and shows that the exporters ranked two to five at the time in combination exported close to 22 percent of the country's buffalo meat (Export Genius 2017). The top-5 companies in other words accounted for around 55 percent of all Indian beef exports. Indications indeed of accumulation patterns with distinct class dynamics.

State-Capital Relations in the Bovine Sector

Relations between Modi's government and this surging industry are, as indicated, strained and uneasy. On the one hand, ongoing transformations in the meat industry align unproblematically with the more general economic restructuring under Modi that favours large-scale capital and its class fractions. On the other hand, in his spectacularly successful 2014 electoral campaign, Modi's authoritarian populist discourse cast the meat industry as a villain, lambasting the incumbent Congress-led government for allowing a "Pink Revolution" in meat, in breach with "Hindu" values. "This country wants a Green Revolution", Modi said, adding that:

> But those at the centre want a Pink Revolution. Do you know what it means? When animals are slaughtered, the colour of their flesh is pink. Animals are being slaughtered and taken out of the country. The government in Delhi is giving subsides to those who are carrying out this slaughter.
>
> (cited in Kumar 2014)

The most striking manifestation of state contradictions involved here is of course the meat industry's continued growth, despite the crackdowns that followed Modi's win. As mentioned, political opponents and other critics have noted this contradiction and have accused Modi of "double standards" including by way of speculations about the alleged involvement of BJP politicians and supporters in the beef export industry (PTI 2018). One such case of speculation that was publicised in 2015 held BJP MLA Sangeet Som, a noted anti-beef consumption advocate (who was incidentally also accused in the Hindutva fuelled riots in Muzaffarnagar in 2013), to have been involved in a land deal for a new meat facility for the company Al Dua Food Processing Pvt Ltd. This company was listed in 2017 as the country's sixth largest export company, a company in which Som also earlier held a directorial post. Som denied all allegations (Rai 2015). Reports about Allanasons investing crores of Rupees to develop the village of Jayapur in Modi's constituency in Uttar Pradesh have in a comparable manner fuelled speculations about unsavoury close ties between India's leading beef exporter and the Modi regime (Singh 2022). So too has newspaper documentation from 2015 that subsidiaries of Allanasons had donated INR 2.5 crore to the BJP for an election campaign

(Dhawan 2015). Given the opaque ways in which money flows in Indian politics (Kapur and Vaishnav 2018), this indicates the existence of larger unreported transactions between big players in the meat industry, and BJP politicians and governments.

The state contradiction between the political Hindutva "moment" of Modi's authoritarian populism and its intertwined neoliberalising economic "moment" manifest elsewhere too. As we described in our introduction, unfazed by accusations of double standards, Modi's government has recognised and rewarded Allanasons for outstanding export performance and its overall contributions to the food sector. The company's Director Fauzan Alavi also sits on National Human Rights Commission as a special monitor for the environment since 2022. And, in the policy domain the government subsidy for slaughterhouses increased by 33 per cent during Modi's first term in power, despite his strong criticism of his predecessor's excessively subsidised pink revolution (Sharma 2019). This increase in subsidies came under the central government-run scheme of the National Mission for Food Processing, introduced in 2014, aiming to upgrade and modernise slaughtering facilities, as part of a broader thrust towards modernising supply chains for ease of capital flows in agro-industrial sectors, with an emphasis on food processing including meat. This, we would argue, resonates with Modi's broad "Make in India" agenda, which includes streamlining and upgrading processing facilities and value chains across different sectors. India's food processing sector was indeed in 2019 recognised by the USDA (2019) as a "sunrise sector" with great potential for capital investment, a sign of a certain interest from international capital, although – and counter to what Modi's regime rhetorically claims under the "Make in India" umbrella – one should be wary of overestimating the flow of investments into a broadly stagnating Indian economy (see, e.g. Mody 2023). All in all, the agro-industrial reform favoured by Modi's government pushes towards capital-intensive and increasingly integrated operations – making for a specific trajectory of agrarian change tying up with specific class and accumulation dynamics.

Perhaps the clearest indicator of continuing meat export expansion under Modi is the concerted efforts at agreements with China for direct imports of Indian meat. These efforts have been ongoing since 2014, described by an (anonymous) leading government official as a "top priority" (Mathew 2017), alongside efforts at controlling foot and mouth disease in the livestock herd, to fulfil regulations in China. This effort was described in newspapers as one of the first actions taken by Modi's second government in 2019 (Pandey 2019). However, in late 2019, crackdowns in China on trade of buffalo from Vietnam (but mostly originating from India) put this lucrative business at risk, ostensibly leading to speculations on the Indian side about shifting towards Indonesia as a possible step-in market (Parija 2019; Parija and Srivastava 2020), while also working to enlist Brazil as a new potential collaborator (KNN India 2020). The list of indications of the continuing drive towards export expansion is long, in other words, and also includes leading industry representatives confidently contemplating "stepping in" to meet global beef shortages caused by the COVID-19 crisis that severely hit global meat production and trade, something that we return to at greater length in chapter four.

Conclusion

Bovine politics and various forms of cow protectionism have emerged as key aspects of the political landscape under Modi's authoritarian populism, simultaneously playing out in the legal sphere of ever-tightening regulations surrounding bovines and in the extra-legal sphere of cow vigilantism – and tacitly or overtly supported by the state. Proceeding from an analysis of the significance of bovines and bovine symbolism to Hindu nationalist politics, this chapter has analysed the ways by which the dual nature of bovine politics and cow protectionism unfolds in Modi's India. While new legal instruments have in their own right imposed strong restrictions on the transport and slaughter of cows and cattle, they have at the same time constituted powerful tools for Hindu nationalist vigilante groups of "cow protectionists" to seek out, discipline, and violently punish Muslims in the cattle trade – the quintessential "threatening Other" of Hindu nationalism. Yet we have also insisted that any such account of the political moment of Modi's authoritarian populism would be partial – and hence misleading – unless coupled with an equally incisive interest in the economic counterpart with which it is inextricably intertwined. Our account of the bovine economy worked from the observation that the surge in violent attention to beef eating under Modi is paralleled in a contradictory way by a dramatic surge in beef exports. Unravelling the political economy of India's beef agro-industry, we find processes of change that are much less publicised than violent Hindutva vigilantism, namely a profound restructuring propelled by Modi's neoliberal economic policies by which an informal bovine economy largely in the hands of classes of labour in the countryside faces aggressive usurping competition from a rising formal agro-industry that is centralised, capital intensive and firmly controlled by dominant class interests. This industry, we have shown, sits in an uneasy yet intimate proximity to Modi's regime, exemplifying Poulantzas' state contradictions most clearly. Following Bernstein (2020) and McKay and colleagues (2020), we suggest that this needs to be interpreted as evidence of the contradictory dynamics of capital accumulation and class underlying Modi's authoritarian populism. The following chapters seek to explore the consequences of these unfolding dynamics. We proceed, in the next chapter, to analyse how the key central contradiction plays out in real life among classes of labour involved in the bovine economy in the Indian countryside and cities, revealing their decidedly negative and destructive consequences.

Notes

1. This and the following sections draw partly on Jakobsen and Nielsen (2021).
2. Existing legislation may be accessed at: https://cjp.org.in/cow-slaughter-prevention-laws-in-india/
3. The fact that this includes non-BJP states indicates the hegemonic position of cow protectionism in the Indian polity today, and the capacity of Modi's authoritarian populism in shaping political common sense.
4. The introduction of cow protection laws may at times produce internal conflicts within the BJP. For example, new legislation in Maharashtra and Karnataka have raised concerns about a potential beef shortage in neighbouring Goa which – with an electorally significant population of Christians and Muslims – consumes large amounts of beef. This has led Goa's BJP chief minister to take steps to ensure that the state is not hit by an "indirect beef ban", and that beef supply remains stable. Northeast India, where beef eating remains common, presents another complicated political scenario for the BJP, which has often toned down or side-lined the more uncompromising aspects of cow protectionism there (Longkumer 2021). Yet irrespective of such contradictions within the BJP's Hindu nationalist project, the outcome has nevertheless overall been the steadfast profusion of legislative protections across the country.
5. Human Rights Watch (2019) reports how the Haryana government, for example, in 2016, "set up a 24-hour helpline for citizens to report cow slaughter and smuggling, and appointed police task forces to respond to the complaints".
6. The drop in exports between 2018 and 2020 is attributable to dramatically reduced exports to Vietnam and, as we elaborate on in chapter four, the impact of COVID-19.
7. Data retrieved from https://resourcetrade.earth
8. Data retrieved from: Per capita meat consumption by type, 2020 (ourworldindata.org)
9. See report at http://apeda.gov.in/apedawebsite/MEAT_MANUAL/Chap1/chap1.pdf
10. See report at http://mospi.nic.in/sites/default/files/publication_reports/nss_rep_572.pdf
11. The link between dairy and industrial killing of bovines is however largely ignored by cow protection legislation (Narayanan 2019).
12. This points to complex class/caste relations at work in the meat industry, where the very notion of "dominant class" interests would need further unpacking through sustained empirical research into the key actors in the industry.
13. The utilisation of such "trolls" is indeed a key frontline for the cultural politics of the contemporary Hindutva movement, registered across various domains as a deliberate social media strategy.
14. See website http://apeda.gov.in/apedawebsite/SubHead_Products/Buffalo_Meat.htm
15. Uttar Pradesh likely also procures animals from neighboring states (Landes et al. 2016).

References

Adcock, C. 2019. "Preserving and Improving the Breeds": Cow Protection's Animal-Husbandry Connection. *South Asia: Journal of South Asian Studies* 42 (6): 1141–1155.

Ahmad, Z. 2013. Marginal Occupations and Modernising Cities: Muslim Butchers in Urban India. *Economic and Political Weekly* 48 (32): 121–131.

Anand, M. 2014. "Pink Revolution" Beneficial to Whom? *Open,* 20 October, http://www.openthemagazine.com/article/india/pink-revolution-beneficial-to-whom

Andersen, W., and Damle, S. D. 2019. *Messengers of Hindu Nationalism: How the RSS Reshaped India.* London: Hurst.

Bernstein, H. 2020. Unpacking "Authoritarian Populism" and Rural Politics: Some Comments on ERPI. *Journal of Peasant Studies* 47 (7): 1526–1542.

Borras, S. M. 2020. Agrarian Social Movements: The Absurdly Difficult but Not Impossible Agenda of Defeating Right-wing Populism and Exploring a Socialist Future. *Journal of Agrarian Change* 20 (1): 3–36.

Business Standard. 2019. Cow Slaughter Act: Haryana Govt Gives Nod to Stricter Provisions. 25 June, https://www.business-standard.com/article/pti-stories/cow-slaughter-act-haryana-govt-gives-nod-to-stricter-provisions-119062500941_1.html

Chakraborty, A. 2017. India's Biggest Buff Meat Exporter Gets Govt Award for "Outstanding Performance". *News18,* 14 June, https://www.news18.com/news/india/indias-biggest-buff-meat-exporter-gets-govt-award-for-outstanding-performance-1432427.html

Copland, I. 2014. History in Flux: Indira Gandhi and the "Great All-Party Campaign" for the Protection of the Cow, 1966–8. *Journal of Contemporary History* 49 (2): 410–439.

Daniyal, S. 2020. At a Time of Acute Farmer Distress, Karnataka's Bovine Slaughter Bill Will Make Lives Even Worse. *Scroll,* 25 August, https://scroll.in/article/981255/at-a-time-of-acute-farmer-distress-karnataka-s-bovine-slaughter-bill-will-make-lives-even-worse

Deccan Herald. 2020. Earlier, Cow Vigilantes Were at Risk: Karnataka Deputy CM Ashwath Naryan on Anti-Cow-Slaughter Law. 11 December, https://www.deccanherald.com/india/karnataka/earlier-cow-vigilantes-were-at-risk-karnataka-deputy-cm-ashwath-naryan-on-anti-cow-slaughter-law-926045.html

Dhawan, H. 2015. BJP Got Rs. 2.50 cr in Donations from Firms Exporting Buffalo Meat. *The Times of India,* 16 December, https://timesofindia.indiatimes.com/india/BJP-got-Rs-2-50-cr-in-donations-from-firms-exporting-buffalo-meat/articleshow/50195323.cms

Dorin, B., and Landy, F. 2009. *Agriculture and Food in India: A Half-century Review from Independence to Globalization.* New Delhi: Manohar.

Eakin, E. 2002. Holy Cow a Myth? An Indian Finds the Kick Is Real. *The New York Times,* 17 August, https://www.nytimes.com/2002/08/17/books/holy-cow-a-myth-an-indian-finds-the-kick-is-real.html

Export Genius. 2017. Top Beef Exporters in India: Report on Beef and Other Meat Exporters. *Export Genius Blog,* 6 May, https://www.exportgenius.in/blog/top-beef-exporters-in-india-report-on-beef-and-other-meat-exporters-22.php

FICCI. 2013. *Overview of the Indian Buffalo Meat Value Chain.* New Delhi: FICCI.

Fischer, J. 2023. *Vegetarianism, Meat and Modernity in India.* London: Routledge.

Freitag, S. B. 1980. Sacred Symbol as Mobilizing Ideology: The North Indian Search for a "Hindu" Community. *Comparative Studies in Society and History* 22 (4): 597–625.

Gittinger, J. L. 2017. The Rhetoric of Violence, Religion, and Purity in India's Cow Protection Movement. *Journal of Religion and Violence* 5 (2): 131–150.

Govindrajan, R. 2018. *Animal Intimacies: Interspecies Relatedness in India's Central Himalayas.* Chicago, IL: Chicago University Press.

Hardy, K. C. 2019. Provincialising the Cow: Buffalo–Human Relationships. *South Asia: Journal of South Asian Studies* 42 (6): 1156–1172

HRW. 2019. Violent Cow Protection in India: Vigilante Groups Attack Minorities. *HRW*, 18 February, https://www.hrw.org/report/2019/02/19/violent-cow-protection-india/vigilante-groups-attack-minorities

Ilaiah Shepherd, K. 2019. Freedom to Eat. *The Caravan*, 1 November, https://caravanmagazine.in/reportage/fight-beef-democratic-right

India Times. 2017. What Goes on Inside the Mind of a Gau-rakshak and How Cows Make His World Go Round! 24 April, https://www.indiatimes.com/news/what-goes-on-inside-the-mind-of-a-gau-rakshak-and-how-cows-make-his-world-go-round-276314.html

Jaffrelot, C. 2019. A *De Facto* Ethnic Democracy? Obliterating and Targeting the Other, Hindu Vigilantes, and the Ethno-State. In *Majoritarian State: How Hindu Nationalism Is Changing India*, edited by Chatterji, A. P., Hansen, T. B. and Jaffrelot, C., 41–67. London: Hurst.

Jaffrelot, C. 2021. *Modi's India: Hindu Nationalism and the Rise of Ethnic Democracy*. Princeton, NJ: Princeton University Press.

Jakobsen, J. 2020. The Maize Frontier in Rural South India: Exploring the Everyday Dynamics of the Contemporary Food Regime. *Journal of Agrarian Change* 20 (1): 137–162.

Jakobsen, J., and Hansen, A. 2020. Geographies of Meatification: An Emerging Asian Meat Complex. *Globalizations* 17 (1): 93–109.

Jakobsen, J., and Nielsen, K. B. 2021. Bovine Contradictions: The Politics of (De)-Meatification and Hindutva Hegemony in Neoliberal India. In *Changing Meat Cultures: Food Practices, Global Capitalism and the Consumption of Animals*, edited by Hansen, A. and Syse, K. L., 121–141. Lanham, MD: Rowman and Littlefield.

Jha, D. N. 2002. *The Myth of the Holy Cow*. London: Verso.

Jha, D. K. 2017. *Shadow Armies: Fringe Organizations and Foot Soldiers of Hindutva*. Delhi: Juggernaut Books.

Kapur, D., and Vaishnav, M. (eds). 2018. *Costs of Democracy: Political Finance in India*. Oxford: Oxford University Press.

Khan, A. A., and Bidabadi, F. S. 2004. Livestock Revolution in India: Its Impact and Policy Response. *South Asia Research* 24 (2): 99–122.

KNN India. 2020. IIA Invites Brazil to be Country Partner for "India Food Expo 2020". 25 January, https://knnindia.co.in/news/newsdetails/global/iia-invites-brazil-to-be-country-partner-for-india-food-expo-2020

Kumar, R. 2014. Modi Targets "Pink Revolution". *The Telegraph*, 3 April, https://www.telegraphindia.com/india/modi-targets-pink-revolution/cid/191376

Landes, M., Melton, A., and Edwards, S. 2016. *From Where the Buffalo Roam: India's Beef Exports*. Washington, DC: United States Department of Agriculture.

Longkumer, A. 2021. *The Greater India Experiment: Hindutva and the Northeast*. Stanford, CA: Stanford University Press.

Manor, J. 2019. Can Modi and the BJP Achieve and Sustain Hegemony? In *Majoritarian State: How Hindu Nationalism is Changing India*, edited by Chatterji, A. P., Hansen, T. B. and Jaffrelot, C., 117–130. London: Hurst.

Mathew, L. 2017. China Finally Agrees to Import Buffalo Meat From India. *The Indian Express*, 16 January, https://indianexpress.com/article/business/business-others/china-finally-agrees-to-import-buffalo-meat-from-india-4476301/

McKay, B. M., Oliveira, G. de L. T., and Liu, J. 2020. Authoritarianism, Populism, Nationalism and Resistance in the Agrarian South. *Canadian Journal of Development Studies/Revue Canadienne d'études du Développement* 41 (3): 347–362.

Metcalf, B., and Metcalf, T. 1998. *A Concise History of Modern India*. Cambridge: Cambridge University Presss.

Mody, A. 2023. India's Boom Is a Dangerous Myth. *Project Syndicate*, 29 March, https://www.project-syndicate.org/commentary/india-economy-boom-is-a-myth-actually-failing-most-people-by-ashoka-mody-2023-03

Nair, K. N. 1981. Review: Studies on India's Cattle Economy. *Economic and Political Weekly* 16 (9): 321–323.

Narayanan, Y. 2018. Cow Protection as "Casteised Speciesism": Sacralisation, Commercialisation and Politicisation. *South Asia: Journal of South Asian Studies* 41(2): 331–351.

Narayanan, Y. 2019. Jugaad and Informality as Drivers of India's Cow Slaughter Economy. *Environment and Planning A: Economy and Space* 51 (7): 1516–1535.

Narayanan, Y. 2023. *Mother Cow, Mother India: A Multispecies Politics of Dairy in India*. Stanford, CA: Stanford University Press.

Natrajan, B. 2018. Cultural Identity and Beef Festivals: Toward a "Multiculturalism against Caste". *Contemporary South Asia* 26 (3): 287–304.

Natrajan, B., and Jacob, S. 2018. "Provincialising" Vegetarianism: Putting Indian Food Habits in Their Place. *Economic and Political Weekly* 53 (9): 54–64.

Nielsen, K. B., and Nilsen, A. G. 2021. Love Jihad and the Governance of Gender and Intimacy in Hindu Nationalist Statecraft. *Religions* 12: 1068.

Nielsen, K. B., and Nilsen, A. G. 2022. Hindu Nationalist Statecraft and Modi's Authoritarian Populism. In *Routledge Handbook on Autocratization in South Asia*, edited by Widmalm, S., 92–100. London: Routledge.

Pandey, G. 1981. *Rallying Round the Cow: Sectarian Strife in the Bhojpur Region, c. 1888–1917*. CSSSC Occasional Paper No. 39. Calcutta: CSSSC.

Pandey, N. 2019. Modi Govt Plans to Push Buffalo Meat Exports as China is Set to Lift Curbs on Indian Beef. *The Print*, 15 July, https://theprint.in/india/governance/modi-govt-plans-to-push-buffalo-meat-exports-as-china-is-set-to-lift-curbs-on-indian-beef/262316/

Parija, P. 2019. China's Crackdown on Illegal Meat Puts India's $2-bn Trade at Risk. *Business Standard*, 9 December, https://www.business-standard.com/article/economy-policy/china-s-crackdown-on-illegal-meat-puts-india-s-2-bn-trade-at-risk-119120900078_1.html

Parija, P., and Srivastava, S. 2020. Top Buffalo Meat Shipper India Keen to Fill Global Shortage. *Bloomberg Quint*, 11 May, https://www.bqprime.com/global-economics/top-buffalo-meat-shipper-india-keen-to-fill-global-shortage

Parikh, A., and Miller, C. 2019. Holy Cow! Beef Ban, Political Technologies, and Brahmanical Supremacy in Modi's India. *ACME: An International Journal for Critical Geographies* 18 (4): 835–874.

Patel, R. 2018. Islamophobia Gastronomica – On the Food Police, Rural Populism and Killing. *Open Democracy*, 26 February, https://www.opendemocracy.net/openIndia/raj-patel/islamophobia-gastronomica-on-food-police-rural-populism-and-killing

Press Information Bureau Delhi. 2021. Livestock Products Exports Increase by 106 % During April-June, 2021–22 in Comparison to April-June, 2020–21 From Rs.

3668 Crores to Rs. 7543 Crores. 28 July, https://pib.gov.in/PressReleasePage.aspx?PRID=1739979

PTI. 2018. Beef Export Flourishing under PM Modi's Regime: Ramalinga Reddy. *Deccan Herald*, 31 March, https://www.deccanherald.com/content/667682/beef-export-flourishing-pm-modis.html

Rai, S. 2015. Al Dua Food Processing Pvt Ltd Says All 3 Directors Muslim, BJP MLA Has Nothing to do With It. *Times of India*, 9 October, https://timesofindia.indiatimes.com/city/meerut/al-dua-food-processing-pvt-ltd-says-all-3-directors-muslim-bjp-mla-has-nothing-to-do-with-it/articleshow/49293722.cms

Ramdas, S. R. 2017a. The Beef Ban Effect: Stray Cattle, Broken Markets and Boom Time for Buffaloes. *The Wire*, 6 April, https://thewire.in/politics/beef-ban-cattle-market

Ramdas, S. R. 2017b. The Sordid Truth About the BJP's Drive Against Meat in UP. *The Wire*, 8 April, https://thewire.in/politics/up-illegal-meat-bjp

Ramdas, S. R. 2020. Will Karnataka's New Bill Sound the Death Knell for Its Cattle Wealth? *The Leaflet*, 15 December, https://www.theleaflet.in/will-karnatakas-new-bill-sound-the-death-knell-for-its-cattle-wealth/#

Safi, M. 2016. On Patrol With the Hindu Vigilantes Who Would Kill to Protect India's Cows. *The Guardian*, 27 October, https://www.theguardian.com/world/2016/oct/27/on-patrol-hindu-vigilantes-smuggling-protect-india-cows-kill

Scholten, B. A. 2010. *India's White Revolution: Operation Flood, Food Aid and Development*. London: IB Tauris.

Sharma, M. 2019. Modi Slammed UPA for Subsidising Slaughterhouses, But His Govt Gave them 33% More Money. *The Print*, 5 December, https://theprint.in/india/governance/modi-slammed-upa-for-subsidising-slaughterhouses-but-his-govt-gave-them-33-more-money/329800/

Singh, P. 2022. Smart Village No. 1, Jayapur. *Outlook India*, 4 February, https://www.outlookindia.com/website/story/smart-village-no-1-jayapur/293913

Srinivas, A. 2018. No, Vegetarianism is Not Growing in India. *Livemint*, 9 October, https://www.livemint.com/Politics/dWUqT4epdPTHNAYuKYVThK/No-vegetarianism-is-not-growing-in-india.html

Staples, J. 2020. *Sacred Cows and Chicken Manchurian: The Everyday Politics of Eating Meat in India*. Seattle, WA: University of Washington Press.

Taskin, B. 2023. From Force-feeding People Dung to Livestreamed "Raids" – Rise of Cow Vigilantism & Monu Manesar. *The Print*, 18 February, https://theprint.in/india/from-force-feeding-people-dung-to-livestreamed-raids-rise-of-cow-vigilantism-monu-manesar/1380796/

USDA. 2019. *India's Food Processing Sector: A Sunrise Sector*. Washington, DC: USDA. https://apps.fas.usda.gov/newgainapi/api/report/downloadreportbyfilename?filename=Food%20Processing%20Ingredients_New%20Delhi_India_5-7-2019.pdf

Vij, S. 2016. Is Jealousy the Reason for Hindutva's Biryaniphobia? *HuffPost*, 7 September, https://www.huffpost.com/archive/in/entry/is-jealousy-the-reason-for-hindutvas-biryaniphobia_in_5c110399e4b0ad8bf05d10dd

Weis, T. 2013. *The Ecological Hoofprint: The Global Burden of Industrial Livestock*. New York: Zed Books.

3 The "Double Victimisation" of Classes of Labour in Countryside and City

In an article on *The Conversation* in 2017, the political scientist Afroz Alam (2017) claimed that "cow economics are killing India's working class". Alam's statement was based on observations from Uttar Pradesh of how the crackdown on the bovine economy there had had severe negative impacts on the urban working classes among Muslims and Dalits, in particular, especially those who laboured in or otherwise depended on the meat or leather sector. In this chapter, we take our cue from Alam's argument as we analyse the ramification for rural lives and livelihoods of India's "right-wing deepening" under Modi. In other words, we analyse the impact of the bovine politics and economics of Modi's authoritarian populism on India's classes of labour, predominantly in the countryside but also in urban and semi-urban contexts. In doing so, we return to some of the key concerns within the Emancipatory Rural Politics Initiative that we discussed in the introduction. We draw in particular upon Bernstein's (2020: 1539) intervention that argues for the need for going beyond a discursive emphasis in studies of authoritarian populism to also ask what class interests it serves, by what means, and with what effects. This chapter seeks to shed light on the last of these questions in particular.

The notion of classes of labour is crucial to our analysis. Coined by Bernstein (2006), the term classes of labour "refers to all those who share a position as members of directly and indirectly exploited classes" (Pattenden 2023: 6). Classes of labour rely on a mix of livelihood strategies, dependent on wage labour, often in combination with petty commodity production such as farming for markets. Yet while these strategies may enable simple reproduction, they do not enable accumulation. The notion of classes of labour opens for examining agrarian change as a process of antagonistic class relations, in which dominant classes stand opposed to classes of labour as exploiters, something Pattenden has shown to be a greatly efficient analytic for exploring patterns of agrarian change in contemporary India (Pattenden 2016; see also Bose 2023). It opens, moreover, for a view of agrarian change that does not artificially and unhelpfully distinguish "peasants" from wage labourers, but approaches classes of labour as a differentiated category encompassing the breadth of livelihoods strategies that are representative of inhabitants of rural, semi-urban as well as urban parts of the Global South and beyond, where "most have to pursue their means of livelihood/reproduction across different sites of the social division of labour: urban and rural, agricultural and non-agriculture, wage employment and self-employment" (Bernstein 2006: 455). This characterisation is highly illuminating of patterns of employment in contemporary India. For the last 20 years – since the 2003 round of the National Sample Survey Organisation (NSSO) – we have known that smallholders have difficulties reproducing their households economically. As Shah and Harriss-White (2011: 15) have pointed out, the average income for farmers operating less than four hectares of land was in fact shown by the 2003 NSSO data to be negative. As a consequence, multiple livelihood options are now necessary for the reproduction of rural households, with wage labour in its manifold shapes assuming an increasingly crucial position in a rural population where the majority, in effect, make a living as "farmer-labourers" (Lerche 2021). Lastly, the concept of classes of labour points towards the characteristic fragmentation underway among the working people of the world. This has profound political implications (see Pattenden 2023), as we emphasise in our discussion of the potential for counter-hegemonic mobilisation and the emergence of progressive politics in the countryside in our concluding chapter.

We base our analysis in this chapter on media reports and investigative journalism, predominantly from the period 2014 to 2019, that is, from Modi's first term as Prime Minister. As shown in the previous chapter, this was a particularly repressive phase in contemporary Indian bovine politics, both in terms of the level of violent vigilantism and with regards to legislative tightening. In contrast, during Modi's second term in office, and particularly following the onset of the COVID-19 pandemic in 2020, political attention for a time shifted elsewhere. While the post-COVID-19 period is the focus of the next chapter, this chapter seeks to demonstrate that a key impact of Modi's authoritarian populism as it has played out in the domains of bovine politics and economics has been what we refer to as the double victimisation of certain groups of classes of labour. These groups of classes of labour are the direct and indirect victims of new forms of legal and extra-legal regulation that restrict economic agency and produce economic hardship and physical suffering. At the same time, these groups are increasingly excluded from a transforming bovine economy because of broader political-economic restructuring that favours dominant class interests. Insofar as the Modi regime depends upon – and has hitherto been remarkably efficient at – incorporating broad sections of the population including classes of labour, the double victimisation that we analyse in this chapter potentially has significant consequences for the continued reproduction of Modi's authoritarian populism in coming years.

Rural Classes of Labour and the Value of Bovines

As discussed earlier, the average "herd size" for bovines in India is as little as two animals, with livestock-rearing most common among households with "marginal" and "small" landholdings and landless households. Such households use cattle in mixed farming systems for transport, grazing, fertilisation, and dairy, thereby opening multiple avenues for income. Selling cattle once the lactation or reproductive age is over usually recovers 30–40 percent of the cost of a new milk-yielding animal and is crucial to the social reproduction of rural classes of labour. It is similarly common for farmers to sell their draught animals soon after the main agriculture season is over, and then re-invest in a new pair of animals for the next season. If robust beef, offals and leather markets are in place, sold animals will command between one-fourth and one-third of its original price. In the case of female cattle, farmers usually sell their fourth or fifth lactation females, which may be transported to states permitting slaughter. Money from the sale would be used to partially offset the cost of a new animal (Salve 2020). Among poor families, the capture and selling of stray cattle to butchers has sometimes provided a source of income. In drought-affected areas – such as parts of Maharashtra, Karnataka, Madhya Pradesh, and Uttar Pradesh – where rural classes of labour live precarious lives, cattle may also be sold simply to tide over economic crises (Singh 2017). Such crises are indeed ever-more present in the lives of India's rural classes of labour. The last couple of decades have seen agrarian livelihoods in India undergoing processes of intensifying precarity and indebtedness, a development that is frequently discussed in terms of the country's ongoing "agrarian crisis" of agricultural stagnation, compounded by climate change (see Jakobsen 2018; Lerche 2013; Vasavi 2012). The declining profitability of crop production is central to this development, leading to increased dependence among rural classes of labour on non-crop income streams to patch together a minimum livelihood. As noted earlier, already a decade ago livestock had surpassed crop production in terms of monetary contribution to the Indian economy (Mahapatra 2012). In the typical language of economists, livestock are therefore now increasingly described as a "living bank" for rural households as they have to manoeuvre economic crises and hardships that are multiplying, intensifying, and accelerating. Given that Indian agriculture has become much more of a "gamble" where the risks are high (Matthan 2022; Münster 2015), the livestock "bank" has become ever more crucial to the livelihoods of classes of labour.

The Shrinking of a Bovine Economy

The bovine politics of India's Hindu nationalists therefore impacts an agrarian context that is already highly vulnerable, with considerable compounding ramifications. The broader pattern is one where cow vigilantism and new legal restrictions imposed on the transport and slaughter of cattle have in effect amounted to a comprehensive clampdown on the cattle trade, the partial collapse of animal markets, and a concomitant inability of classes of labour to dispose of their cattle in economically sensible ways. Even in places where sales formally remain legal, the violence of vigilante groups has instilled fear among rural classes of labour who often no longer dare to sell their buffaloes or aged milk-yielding cattle for fear of reprisals. Unable to dispose of cattle in economically sound ways, they are faced with the additional economic and labour burden that maintaining aged and unproductive animals entails, as these need feeding, grazing, watering, cleaning, and healthcare (Salve 2020). Estimates suggest that the maintenance of one aged and unproductive cattle can be as much as INR 6,000 per month (Mander 2023; Narayanan 2023: 153), a sum that – if correctly calculated – would constitute almost the entire average monthly income of a person living in India's poorer states. An additional expense of this magnitude evidently affects rural classes of labour disproportionately. Within the broad category of classes of labour, we find that Dalits and Muslims have been particularly victimised (Ramdas 2020a) – an unsurprising finding given that the majority of the approximately 20 million workers involved in India's beef trade come from these communities.

In the following, we identify variants of this broader pattern in key Indian states where the impact of the bovine politics and economics of Modi's authoritarian populism has been the strongest. This includes the western state of Maharashtra, the northern states of Haryana, Rajasthan, and Uttar Pradesh, in particular, as well as in the southern state of Karnataka.

In Maharashtra, the targeting of the bovine economy has been felt hard. Writing five years after the stricter legal provisions criminalising the slaughter of cattle had been introduced, Ramdas (2020b) argued that this had, in effect, destroyed Maharashtra's diverse cattle economy:

> Maharashtra's rich beef food cultures and associated post-slaughter wealth of cattle skin, hide and leather has been central towards sustaining cattle populations and are the basis for the re-sale value of unproductive animals. Once banned, the sustainable cycle of production it supported, collapsed, and farmers stopped rearing cattle.
>
> (Ramdas 2020b)

The production cycles of purchase and sales of animals, crucial both for farmers' livelihoods and sustaining cattle in the agricultural economy, Ramdas asserts, had effectively collapsed, as had markets for bullocks and cows, causing huge losses and distress to small and marginal farmers in the countryside (Ramdas 2017a, 2020b). A 2015 video that began to circulate on WhatsApp not long after the ban came into effect in a particularly dramatic way illustrates the predicament that many Maharashtra farmers now found themselves in. According to *Deccan Herald*:

> A grim video has been circulating among farmers across the sun-baked plains of Maharashtra travelling from one cell phone to the next via Whats-App. In the video, a man stands with his two trusty bulls at a cattle market. A crowd surrounds him, transfixed by his emphatic lamentations. He cries out that his beasts of burden are old and unable to work and that his meagre savings are nearly gone. He needs to sell the animals, but none of the usual buyers – the Hindu middlemen who sell the bulls to Muslims for slaughter – are buying. Without the money from the old bulls, he says, he will never be able to afford new ones. "How am I supposed to keep farming?" he shouts. "Should I just hang myself here in this market?"
>
> (Bearak 2015)

As the reporter went on to note, the farmer's threat did not ring empty. At the time, this part of the central Indian hinterland had for long witnessed widespread and prolonged agrarian distress, with an average of four farmers taking their own lives every day as a consequence. The desperation of the farmer in the circulated video is, in this context, a tragic indication of how the legal and extra-legal crackdown on beef most severely and most immediately impacted the livelihoods of rural classes of labour.

Even though the legal restrictions on the slaughter and consumption of beef introduced in Maharashtra in 2015 were strict, their sometimes-patchy implementation also illustrates how bovine legislation never has the full power "to create the worlds it seeks to call into being" (Adcock and Govindrajan 2019: 1101). Rather, as Staples writes with specific reference to India's beef bans (2020: 99), the act of making something illegal can often first and foremost function to "determine the parameters within which it continues to happen". According to the Bombay Mutton Dealers' Association, an important outcome of the criminalisation of beef had been that much of the trade had simply moved underground and passed into the hands of "anti-social elements".[1] As a result, thousands of "law-abiding" and formerly "gainfully employed" meat traders who had often been in the trade for generations had been driven out of business. This included sections of the educationally and financially backward caste Muslim Qureshi community of butchers. Many among this community depend on their stigmatised and sensitive occupation (Ahmad 2013: 121) for their livelihoods and are routinely the targets of what Shaheed Tayob (2019) calls a politics of disgust because of their association with animal slaughter – a key element in the dehumanisation of Muslims by Hindu nationalists. When the new legal restrictions were announced, the Qureshi butchers were quick to protest as they feared that "the ban on beef will ruin us", as one butcher put it (Anvekar 2015). But their protests had little impact, and two years later, in 2017, many Qureshi butchers were reportedly still unemployed, or earning very small incomes from the still legal water buffalo business, living what they described as "hand-to-mouth" lives (see also Laliwala, Gurmat, and Dhawan 2023). Families were also withdrawing their children from school – girls in particular – for lack of money (Johari 2017). In addition, as we know from Zarin Ahmad's (2013) work among Qureshi butchers in Delhi, the loss of work entails more than a loss of livelihoods: For Qureshi butchers, working independently has been a means through which to assign honour and prestige, as well as skill and masculinity, to an otherwise highly stigmatised form of work.

The observation that the main effect of making something illegal can sometimes be to redefine the parameters within which it continues to happen also resonates when it comes to the sale of cattle in Maharashtra after the beef ban. While the criminalisation of beef did lead to a very considerable and fear-induced decline in cattle sales – as the desperation of the distressed farmer in the circulated video tragically illustrates – some cattle sales continued to happen, albeit at very reduced levels. However, cattle-owning classes of labour who wanted to sell in order to recuperate some of the value of their aged cattle were increasingly forced into the illegal market where the risks are much greater and options fewer (Ganapatye 2020). With declining availability of beef meat in the market, poor consumers of meat have also been hit hard insofar as beef used to be their cheapest source of protein. There have also been severe repercussions for classes of labour among Maharashtra leatherworkers whose livelihoods are based on the hides, leather, and cattle skins of the post-slaughter economy.

In Rajasthan, raids by cow vigilantes have been regular, often violent, and have in some accounts even been described as "the new normal". Here, journalists have described how villages dependent on the cattle economy are facing economic trouble. A 2019 report on Khoabas village in Alwar district tells of how Muslim villagers who take their cattle 10 kilometres away in search of pasture, are routinely victims of vigilante raids, during which cattle might be forcefully confiscated, and the owner assaulted. As one Muslim victim of vigilante attacks and several random police arrests put it: "From the nurturers of a sound cattle economy, we are now looked at as enemies of the cow. Worse, we have been branded cow smugglers."[2] This scenario has made cattle-rearing virtually impossible and certainly economically unsustainable as keeping the cattle in the relative safety of the village requires prohibitively expensive stall-feeding. This has placed rural households in a situation where they in practice can neither sell their cattle (for fear of reprisals) nor keep it (because of economic constraints). As a way out, villagers have started quitting cattle-rearing altogether, for fear of the rising threat of violence over virtually all forms of cattle movement. This has made the cow almost a "pariah breed". As the reporter Jitendra wrote from Khoabas: "Cattle have simply vanished from the village's landscape. At best, a few households keep some buffaloes or goats. It is like an economic plague taking its victims one at a time, eventually sweeping away everybody." With cattle having almost disappeared from the village, cattle farmers turn to daily wage labour at construction sites in the city. Villagers engaged in dairy farming have also been jailed after being charged with cruelty against animals, and some have given up their business. And there are reports from other villages in Rajasthan that similarly tell of households having withdrawn from the cattle profession, turning to labour migration for daily wages in the city (Jitendra 2019a).

In Haryana, the situation is very similar to that described above from Rajasthan. Here too, stringent laws and vigilantism have forced farmers into a situation where they have to keep unproductive cattle. Reports from the backward Mewat district tell of how not just the trade of bovines, but even the trade of goats – common only among the poorest rural households who combine this activity with casual labour – has reportedly been targeted by the police. At a weekly market in Mewat, about 1,500 cattle and buffaloes used to change hands every week. But following the crackdown on the beef trade, the number of buffaloes (and also goats) coming to the market has drastically reduced as traders keep away due to increased attacks on cattle transporters. Unofficial estimates suggest that the cattle trade has slumped by as much as 80 percent. The pattern is one where Mewat's Muslims – as in Alwar in Rajasthan – are routinely stigmatised as cow slaughterers and smugglers, and where the possession of even small quantities of beef, or simply meat alleged to be beef, has led to attacks, especially on Muslims and Dalits (Jitendra 2019b). A resident Muslim of Mewat told a reporter that he experienced the violence as deliberately aimed at "depriving the villagers of their only source of livelihood – dairy farming". He went on to spell out what he saw as the implications: "It is all a part of a calibrated plan of extermination having features of a small-scale genocide and even ethnic cleansing" (Anwar 2023). A report by Harsh Mander (2023) from 2023 echoed similar sentiments and painted a gloomy picture of the situation in Haryana. Lynchings of Muslims on the suspicion of cow slaughter had produced "an environment of terror", Mander wrote, in which the widespread atmosphere of fear was sustained by a Hindu majoritarian administration with close ties to vigilante gangs operating with an "indestructible sense of impunity and raw power". As a result, most cattle herders had given up rearing cows for fear of reprisals, almost erasing the cow from pastoral life in the state. The lively trade in beef biryani from small roadside carts along highways in Mewat, which had earlier secured employment for thousands of people forming part of classes of labour, had similarly almost disappeared by 2023 due to harassment and repeated raids by the police and vigilante groups in search of illegal cow meat in the biryani.

The "cow smuggling" that villagers in this part of India are frequently accused of and targeted for forms part of a pattern of cattle trade linking western India to Bangladesh via border crossings in West Bengal and Assam, a trade that has a history back to colonial times. More than 2 million cattle are reportedly smuggled across the border annually, an institutionalised practice that is known to involve the active collusion of the police and border security, as well as rural residents in both countries involved in the smuggling supply chain (Javed and Mahato 2023). Increased militarisation of the border under Modi's government has put increased scrutiny on this system, leading among other things to renewed forms of surveillance and repression by state forces upon Muslim Assamese villagers in the border area (Sur 2020). This is further fuelled by persistent political rhetoric from the Hindu right about "well-established links" between funds from the smuggling trade and international (Islamist) terrorism, coupled with occasional demands for the death penalty for cattle smugglers (Govindrajan 2018: 67, 76), and the dismissal of smugglers as cruel and depraved people (Adcock and Govindrajan 2019: 1103). The spectre of cattle smuggling that haunts Muslims in Haryana has meant that cattle traders in different parts of Assam have had to face repeated attacks from vigilante groups who have accused them of smuggling the animals (*India Today* 2017). It has also meant that vigilante groups from Haryana and other parts of North-western India have reportedly taken to sending groups on "missions" to Assam to police the movement of bovines and attack alleged smugglers there (Jeelani 2016).

In Uttar Pradesh, vigilante violence has been particularly intense, and Muslims have been especially targeted to the extent that North India between 2015 and 2017 became "the theatre of a series of lynchings of Muslims, following a near identical pattern each time: The Muslims accused of cattle smuggling or consuming beef were attacked and, in dozens of cases, died of their wounds" (Jaffrelot 2019: 59). While this has had a negative impact on classes of labour comparable to what has been the case in Maharashtra, Rajasthan, and Haryana, the situation in Uttar Pradesh has been further compounded by a move by the state government to close all municipal slaughterhouses in early 2017. Already two years earlier, in 2015, the National Green Tribunal had ordered all slaughterhouses in Uttar Pradesh running without requisite permits to be shut. The state government at the time had ignored this order, but in 2017 the newly elected BJP government – in what was widely seen as a pretext to target the meat industry – decided to enforce the ruling, ordering action against slaughterhouses and meat-sellers operating without valid licences and violating environmental and health rules. This resulted in a virtual shutdown of all government slaughterhouses.

Uttar Pradesh's slaughterhouse ecology is complex and supports diverse social and economic systems and relations, both rural and urban. While the estimate in one report that when one animal is slaughtered 20 people find work, is clearly exaggerated (Moudgil 2017), the closure of Uttar Pradesh's slaughterhouses did impact several million people in direct and indirect ways. The closure of the slaughterhouses in itself directly affected the tens of thousands of people employed there, rendering many unemployed. But it also impacted the entire market chain comprising rural classes of labour with disposable animals, factory and leather workers, and meat sellers and consumers (Ramdas 2017b). The millions of rural agricultural families, mostly with small land holdings or no land at all, who keep cattle for milk, agriculture, or transportation, became unable to fetch good prices for their cattle – even for productive milch cattle, because potential buyers were concerned that they might not be able to resell. And as in Maharashtra, the Qureshi Muslim community of butchers saw their business heavily reduced (Moudgil 2022).

The impact was also felt in allied industries such as leather and meat packaging which in Uttar Pradesh provides formal and informal employment to hundreds of thousands of people. The state houses the largest market for buffalo skin in India, the Pechbagh hide market in Kanpur. This market had seen trade decline since 2015, following the mob lynching of two Muslim men suspected of stealing and slaughtering a stolen cow calf. Hide supplies for the Pechbagh market came largely from the now-closed government abattoirs, while other supplies came from villages through people engaged in skinning dead animals, that is, the Dalit segment of rural classes of labour. Sellers at Pechbagh market reported in mid-2017 that, with municipal abattoirs shut, whatever raw material they now received came exclusively from the villages, and overwhelmingly from animals who died of natural causes (Moudgil 2017). As one tannery owner in Kanpur put it to *The Hindu*: "Now flaying or handling a cow hide is like having a tiger skin, which is totally illegal. Nobody wants to touch the skin of a dead cow; they are too scared" (Cooper 2016). According to another seller, his supply had gone down from 10,000 hides per month to 500, leading to a reduction in number of employees from eight workers to just one (Moudgil 2017). Tannery owners in Kanpur moreover tell a broader story of hardships, in which anti-cow politics compounds other economic challenges, including the recent introduction of new sales taxes. Despite leather being pointed out as a potential growth sector in Modi's flagship "Make in India" programme, one tannery owner held that "you have been left to fend for yourself. I don't know for how long the industry will survive. We will definitely not bring our children into this business" (Chitnis 2017). Crucially, most workers in this sector come from disadvantaged communities. According to one survey, one third of all leather workers are women, while one fourth are scheduled castes and tribes. And, leather workers who are neither from traditional tanning communities nor Muslims tend to come from "poor agricultural families" (Singh 2017), that is, classes of labour in the countryside, including many migrant workers. The crackdown on the bovine economy and the closure of municipal slaughterhouses in Uttar Pradesh, in other words, choked a "small but important revenue stream for its poor farmers, especially in drought-prone areas" where India's classes of labour are especially vulnerable and impoverished (Singh 2017). It also deprived consumers of access to cheap protein in the form of beef meat since the government slaughterhouses were the only source of beef for domestic consumption. Meanwhile, and similar to what we observed above from Maharashtra, the crackdown on the beef economy in Uttar Pradesh has also involved shifts towards underground activities. Illegal cattle trading in the state has been reported to have become institutionalised in ways that depend on the active collusion, through bribery, of the police as well as *gau rakshaks*. According to participants in this illegal trade, the latter benefit financially from these arrangements – reflecting, again, the multiple motivations that drive young men into the cow vigilante groups in the first place, with the lure of quick cash being a noteworthy component (*Tehelka* 2023).

Developments in the southern state of Karnataka in striking ways resemble what has been observed in Uttar Pradesh. Here, the Karnataka Prevention of Slaughter and Preservation of Cattle Act, 2020, rendered almost all cattle transactions potentially criminal, making cattle-owning farmers and classes of labour particularly vulnerable. In their report on the adverse impact of this act, Karpagam and Joshi (2021) document the significant damage done to the entire supply chain. Starting from observations at cattle markets, they show how the number of markets has come down dramatically, from several thousand before the law came into effect, to only a few hundred or less. The number of buyers in particular has come down as people stay away for fear of harassment or attacks by vigilante groups now operating with the backing of law. As a result, farmers can no longer get a good price for their unproductive cattle; often they cannot find a buyer at all. This is especially debilitating for landless farmers (Karpagam and Joshi 2021: 19) and other classes of labour. From the cattle markets, the report moves to the transport sector, perhaps the riskiest link in the entire supply trade. With vigilantes operating with the backing of the state government and with an almost free hand, people transporting cattle are extremely vulnerable to physical attacks, but also to police action. Under the new law, the police are empowered to conduct search and seizure operations based on suspicion alone, and to hand over confiscated cattle to care institutions. As mentioned earlier, the law even offers impunity to people acting on their own initiative and "out of good faith" in implementing the law. As a result, many small-scale transporters have either been driven out of business or have left it. Because of this drying up of the supply chain, activities at slaughterhouses have considerably decreased, as have the skin and hide curing units where a large section of Dalit classes of labour find salaried work. This sector is home to both large and small businesses, but as in Uttar Pradesh, small business has been affected the most (Karpagam and Joshi 2021: 35). Labourers have consequently migrated to neighbouring states en masse, according to one source (Sood 2022). Lastly, at the very end of the bovine chain, Karpagam and Joshi report of butcheries and small eateries shutting down or experiencing drastically reduced sales.

The "Stray Cattle Menace"

With small and marginal farmers thus unable to sell their cattle for a profit, and unable to shoulder the expense that comes with stall-feeding unproductive cattle, many choose to simply let them go. As a result, Uttar Pradesh as well as many other states have seen a steep rise in the number of stray cattle, creating what is often described as a "stray cattle menace". Stray cattle may crowd urban areas, disrupt traffic and cause more accidents, and carry and spread various diseases among the urban population. But more importantly they constitute a major threat to farmers' standing crops and cause widespread economic distress among rural classes of labour – many of whom take to sleeping in their fields to prevent stray cows from eating their crops. It is estimated that India has upwards of six million stray cattle. Of these, 1.6 million are found in Uttar Pradesh alone, according to the 2019 livestock census – an increase of 17 percent in the two years since Yogi Adityanath became Chief Minister in 2017. In the rural areas in Sultanpur district in the state, this rise in stray cattle has been so severe that stray animals have "been running amok", forcing farmers to come out and guard their fields in the morning and at night. Traditional scaffoldings have been erected for farmers to sit and keep an eye on stray animals. Those who can afford it have taken to using barbed wires to keep stray bovines at bay, but this is a costly investment that is mostly out of reach for rural classes of labour. In Siddharthnagar district, villagers complain that destruction to crops caused by stray bovines had increased after 2017 to such an extent that it has become difficult for the local people to survive (Mishra 2022). Fodder has also become more expensive as farmers have changed to non-cereal crops to prevent destruction of crops by stray cattle (Moudgil 2022).

A report from Semri village close to Uttar Pradesh's border with Nepal similarly testifies to the magnitude of the threat of stray cattle to small farmers, but also to a certain creativity in their response to it. In Semri, a village meeting decided to round up stray cattle and transport it into Nepal. This operation reportedly cost the villagers INR 37,000 that was spent on hiring 22 tractors carrying 255 stray cattle across the border – accompanied by more than 40 motorcycles carrying over 100 armed residents – where the cattle was abandoned in the Katarniaghat Wildlife Sanctuary, following a violent scuffle with local Nepalese villagers that left many injured. This was no isolated incident. Many villagers in districts bordering Nepal such as Khiri, Bahraich, and Shravasti, incur great expenses and a considerable risk of violence herding stray cattle across the border (Jitendra 2019c). Elsewhere, farmers have locked up stray cattle in primary schools or other government buildings to protect their crops (*India Times* 2019).

The Political Economy of Gaushalas

Because of the potential political consequences of leaving the stray cattle menace unaddressed, various BJP-led state governments have responded to it through various measures and means. Haryana, for example, proposed to ID-tag all cattle in the state and fine the people who let their cattle loose (*India.com* 2017). Jharkhand reportedly started tagging its cows in 2016 – the same year as the central government announced a plan for spending 500 million rupees at assigning unique 12-digit identity numbers for all the country's millions of cows and bovines (*Firstpost* 2017). In Gujarat, the state government in 2023 sought to stem the challenge posed by stray cattle by ordering the castration of 50,000 stray bulls and locking them up in compounds (*Indian Express* 2023). Other representatives of the Hindu nationalist movement have encouraged farmers to keep their unproductive cows and make money from the production and sale of beauty and health products made from cow dung and urine, an idea that finds a great deal of popular support within the Hindu right, but also beyond (Govindrajan 2018: 63).

More commonly, however, the Hindu nationalist solution to the damage inflicted on India's rural classes of labour by stray cattle has been to set up *gaushalas*, or cow care centres, for aged or unproductive cows. While the official purpose of these gaushalas is to care for such cows until they die a natural death (Sharma 2017), they also function, as Yamini Narayanan (2019) has argued, as sites of "Hindutva ultranationalism", where the "Hindu mother cow" is offered sanctuary, ostensibly from "predatory Muslim males" that would otherwise have killed and consumed her.

Narayanan's (2023) research into the practice of the Simhachalam Temple Gaushalas in Andhra Pradesh offers an illuminating and highly critical perspective on the institution of *gaushalas* more generally. As is common, this *gaushala* was reserved exclusively for indigenous Indian "pure" cow breeds that are associated with Brahmanism, and it rejected both the "foreign" crossbreeds as well as buffaloes (Narayanan 2018, 2023). Most animals that came to the *gaushala* were discarded animals from dairying, but somewhat paradoxically perhaps, the *gaushala* itself largely operated as a dairy farm, producing sacred milk for use in ritual Hinduism. The fact that the *gaushala* was heavily invested in dairying, in turn, meant that it had little use for those male calves and other unwanted animals that arrived. These animals were therefore often sold or traded by the *gaushala*. This practice entailed a good deal of wilful or strategic ignorance on the part of the institution as many of the animals thus sold or traded would soon end up in a slaughterhouse (see also Staples 2019): "Donating bull calves to a temple is a euphemism for sending them to slaughter", as one of Narayanan's (2023: 150) interlocutors phrased it. Other *gaushalas* that Narayanan (ibid.: 172) visited, especially in urban areas, presented a disturbing scenario, their intensely confined spaces serving "literally as sites of overcrowded, lifetime confinement" of cows under appalling conditions (see also Patel 2017).

Other analyses of *gaushalas* bring to light other aspects of their political economy. One report from Haryana (Mander 2023) points to an extortionist nexus between vigilante groups and local *gaushalas* where the former coercively confiscate cows from Muslim dairy farmers and subsequently "donate" them to the latter. The *gaushala* may later offer to return the cow to its rightful owner, but only if it is sufficiently "compensated for the upkeep up the cow in the *gaushala*" by a sum of money often exceeding the cost of the cow itself.

Similarly, a comprehensive 2017 investigation by Reuters (Siddiqui et al. 2017) showed how several *gaushalas* are in effect transit points where cattle stolen from Muslims by cow vigilantes are dropped off and later either given or sold to Hindu farmers. Two of the largest organisations running *gaushalas* in Uttar Pradesh estimated to have confiscated and passed on close to 200,000 cows in a span of just three years after Modi assumed office. Although the market value of seized cattle is hard to estimate, the report suggest that the value of cattle seized by these two organisations in just three years amounts to app. USD 36 million. On average, the 110 *gaushalas* surveyed by Reuters estimated a 50 percent increase in their cattle holding during Modi's first three years in power. In addition, *gaushalas* enjoy increasingly generous state patronage under Modi. It is, for example, estimated that a full 80 percent of the funds granted for animal shelters by the central Animal Welfare Board of India are allocated to *gaushalas* (Narayanan 2023: 146). At the level of the federal states, Haryana's cow protection commission went from allotting INR 18.5 million rupees to cow sheds in 2014–2015, to more than 37 million for 2016–2017. In Rajasthan, funding doubled from about INR one billion in 2013–2014, to more than INR 2.3 billion in 2016–2017 (Siddiqui et al. 2017). A significant part of this money has now been shown to have been granted to "fake *gaushalas*", some of which did not house even a single cow (*OpIndia* 2021). Rajasthan tops the list of states with the most *gaushalas*, with the other North Indian states of Madhya Pradesh, Gujarat, Uttar Pradesh, and Haryana constituting the top-5 (Noronha 2018). And nationally, Modi's central government in 2020 launched a new scheme under which INR 900 crore is set aside for registered *gaushalas* (Shenoy 2020). This political economy of *gaushalas* that are officially presented as a solution to the stray cattle menace, thus entails a considerable state- and corporate-sponsored redistribution of (cattle) wealth from rural classes of labour into the hands of often Hindutva-affiliated groups and organisations.

In tandem with this, *gaushala* maintenance is also becoming a favourite target for corporate CSR spending (Jain and Singh 2018; Mampatta and Kant 2018). The Companies Act, 2013, mandates that firms with a certain net worth, turnover, or net profit must spend at least 2 percent of their average net profit for the preceding three financial years on CSR activities. *Gaushalas* and cattle welfare are included in the list of activities that can be supported, under Schedule VII of the Act. Several large Indian companies have chosen to support such activities. Some companies run their own *gaushala* maintenance projects; some sponsor *gaushala*-related infrastructure development such as constructing drinking waterlines for cattle troughs or overhead tanks for cattle, or weighbridges and fodder storage yards; yet others organise medical camps for cattle or "cattle care camps" (Bhattacharya 2017). A reading by NDTV (Jain and Singh 2018) of select annual reports of top-500 companies on the Bombay Stock Exchange found 11 cases of companies donating money to *gaushalas* to a total of INR 1.42 crore between 2015 and 2017, distributed to 16 different cow shelters. Most of these were located in the northern states of Rajasthan, Haryana, Delhi, and Uttar Pradesh. Among them was the Hanuman Prasad Smarak Samiti Trust in Uttar Pradesh, whose president was the now late Vishnu Hari Dalmia, a key leader of the VHP. CSR spending on *gaushalas* in this way enables large corporate actors to align with the ideological and political agenda of Hindu nationalism, while also channelling corporate profits into activities that alleviate the crackdown-induced stray cattle menace, albeit in a piecemeal way. Piecemeal for the simple reason that *gaushalas* will never be capable of properly "caring for" the hundreds of thousands of bovines that are "discarded" in India every year, and which all require lifelong care (Narayanan 2023: 148).

Conclusion

The analysis and empirics presented in this chapter clearly illustrate how the bovine politics of Hindu nationalism has negatively affected India's classes of labour in both city and countryside, especially but not exclusively Dalits and Muslims, in a very immediate and direct way. It has directly undermined livelihoods and destroyed economic opportunities for classes of labour, while simultaneously reinforcing and aggravating the stigmatisation of the same groups for their association with bovine bodies. While the social, economic, and political emaciation of Muslims and the transformation of India into a Hindu state is of course integral to the political moment of Modi's authoritarian populism, the wider negative impact of this politics on India's complex and extensive bovine economy nevertheless means that the livelihoods of larger sections of India's classes of labour that Modi's regime seeks to incorporate within its hegemonic project are considerably undermined. While segments of this increasingly economically precarious population may be compensated through the "psychological wages" (Nilsen 2023) that flow from their inclusion into the broader project of "Hindu unity" – and sometimes also through the "wages of violence" (Hansen 2001) that accrue to them from their ground-level participation in acts of vigilantism – the situation as analysed in this chapter is one where their incorporation into the political Hindu nationalist project is increasingly at odds with and hostile to their class interests.

To connect the relationship of the political moment of Modi's authoritarian populism more firmly to the economic moment of neoliberalisation, the next chapter proceeds to analyse the consequences for and development of the corporate sector in India's organised beef industry. How and to what extent has this industry been impacted by the legal and extra-legal crackdown on the bovine economy under Modi? This question is at the heart of the next chapter.

Notes

1 Govindrajan (2018: 63) makes a similar observation from Uttarakhand, where a "ban on the transportation and slaughter of cattle pushed the trade in cattle underground and certainly curtailed it but did not succeed in entirely eradicating it".

2 In addition to Muslims, Rajasthan's nomadic-pastoral communities (such as the Banjaras) have frequently been reported as victims of attacks, being also easily singled out for their livestock dependent livelihoods.

References

Adcock, C., and Govindrajan, R. 2019. Bovine Politics in South Asia: Rethinking Religion, Law and Ethics. *South Asia: Journal of South Asian Studies* 42 (6): 1095–1107.

Ahmad, Z. 2013. Marginal Occupations and Modernising Cities: Muslim Butchers in Urban India. *Economic and Political Weekly* 48 (32): 121–131.

Alam, A. 2017. "Cow Economics" Are Killing India's Working Class. *The Conversation*, 22 June, https://theconversation.com/cow-economics-are-killing-indias-working-class-79274

Anvekar, A. 2015. Mumbai: Ban on Beef Will Put All of Us on the Streets, Say Butchers. *Mid-Day*, 4 March, https://www.mid-day.com/mumbai/mumbai-news/article/mumbai--ban-on-beef-will-put-all-of-us-on-the-streets--say-butchers-16034764

Anwar, T. 2023. How Cow Vigilantism Is Hitting Mewat's Dairy Farming Hard. *Newsclick*, 30 March, https://www.newsclick.in/how-cow-vigilantism-hitting-mewats-dairy-farming-hard

Bearak, M. 2015. Maharashtra's Qureshis Lose Out in Beef Ban. *Deccan Herald*, 4 July, https://www.deccanherald.com/opinion/maharashtras-qureshis-lose-out-in-beef-ban-468492.html

Bernstein, H. 2006. Is There an Agrarian Question in the 21st Century? *Canadian Journal of Development Studies/Revue Canadienne d'études du Développement* 27 (4): 449–460.

Bernstein, H. 2020. Unpacking "Authoritarian Populism" and Rural Politics: Some Comments on ERPI. *Journal of Peasant Studies* 47 (7): 1526–1542.

Bhattacharya, R. 2017. Gau Seva Enters India Inc's CSR Stable, Companies Spending Big Money on Cow Upkeep. *The Economic Times*, 14 June, https://economictimes.indiatimes.com/news/politics-and-nation/gau-seva-enters-india-incs-csr-stable-companies-spending-big-money-on-cow-upkeep/articleshow/59134230.cms

Bose, R. 2023. Land, Labour, Dispossession, and Politics among Scheduled Tribes in India: Framing an Adivasi Agrarian Question. Unpublished PhD dissertation, School of International Development, University of East Anglia, UK.

Chitnis, P. 2017. India's Big Job Creating Industry Is Dying a Slow Death. *BQ Prime*, 2 December, https://www.bqprime.com/business/indias-big-job-creating-industry-is-dying-a-slow-death

Cooper, O. 2016. How Does India's Stance on Cattle Slaughter Affect Farmers? *The Cattle Site*, 15 January, https://www.thecattlesite.com/articles/4310/how-does-indias-stance-on-cattle-slaughter-affect-farmers/

Firstpost. 2017. Gau Aadhaar? 88 Million Cows and Buffaloes Across India to Get Unique ID Number. 5 January, https://www.firstpost.com/india/gau-aadhaar-88-mn-cows-and-buffaloes-across-india-to-get-unique-id-number-3189514.html

Ganapatye, S. 2020. Ban on Cattle Slaughter Has Done Little to Stop Beef Trade in Maharasthra. *Mumbai Mirror,* 21 February, https://mumbaimirror.indiatimes.com/mumbai/other/ban-toothless-illegal-beef-trade-thrived-in-5-years/articleshow/74234401.cms

Govindrajan, R. 2018. *Animal Intimacies: Interspecies Relatedness in India's Central Himalayas.* Chicago: Chicago University Press.

Hansen, T. B. 2001. *Wages of Violence: Naming and Identity in Postcolonial Bombay.* Pricenton: Princeton University Press.

India.com. 2017. Haryana to Tag Stray Cattle, Impose Fines. 22 July, https://www.india.com/news/agencies/haryana-to-tag-stray-cattle-impose-fines-2342293/

Indian Express. 2023. To Check Stray Cattle Menace, Gujarat Decides to Castrate 50,000 Bulls. 12 January, https://indianexpress.com/article/cities/gandhinagar/to-check-stray-cattle-menace-gujarat-decides-to-castrate-50000-bulls-8376632/

India Times. 2019. Following Aligarh, Farmers in Agra have Locked Stray Cows in Government School to Protect Crops. 31 January, https://www.indiatimes.com/news/india/following-aligarh-farmers-in-agra-have-locked-stray-cows-in-government-school-to-protect-crops-359565.html

India Today. 2017. Cow Vigilantes Defy PM Modi Yet Again, Attack Drivers Transporting Cattle in Assam. 3 July, https://www.indiatoday.in/india/story/cow-vigilante-guwahati-narendra-modi-1022124-2017-07-03

Jaffrelot, C. 2019. A *De Facto* Ethnic Democracy? Obliterating and Targeting the Other, Hindu Vigilantes, and the Ethno-State. In *Majoritarian State: How Hindu Nationalism is Changing India,* edited by Chatterji, A. P., Hansen, T. B. and Jaffrelot, C., 41–67. London: Hurst.

Jain, S., and Singh, M. P. 2018. India Inc's Donations to Gaushalas Show Surge. *NDTV,* 16 January, https://www.ndtv.com/india-news/india-incs-donations-to-gaushalas-show-surge-ndtv-fact-check-1800408

Jakobsen, J. 2018. Towards a Gramscian Food Regime Analysis of India's Agrarian Crisis: Counter-movements, Petrofarming and Cheap Nature. *Geoforum* 90: 1–10.

Javed, Z., and Mahato, S. 2023. How Millions of Indian Cattle End up in Bangladesh. *The Times of India,* 26 March, https://timesofindia.indiatimes.com/india/how-millions-of-indian-cattle-end-up-in-bangladesh/articleshow/99004187.cms

Jeelani, M. 2016. Till the Cows Come Home in Assam. *The Hindu,* 18 March, https://www.thehindu.com/elections/assam2016/assam-assembly-polls-2016/article8366574.ece

Jitendra. 2019a. India's Cow Crisis Part 2: Threat of Decline Looms Over Livestock Economy after 35 years' Growth. *Down to Earth,* 7 January, https://www.downtoearth.org.in/news/agriculture/india-s-cow-crisis-part-2-threat-of-decline-looms-over-livestock-economy-after-35-years-growth-62731

Jitendra. 2019b. India's Cow Crisis Part 4: The Stigma of Mewat. *Down to Earth,* 10 January, https://www.downtoearth.org.in/news/agriculture/india-s-cow-crisis-part-4-the-stigma-of-mewat-62782

Jitendra. 2019c. India's Cow Crisis Part 1: Nepal Bears the Brunt of India's Cow Vigilantism. *Down to Earth,* 4 January, https://www.downtoearth.org.in/news/agriculture/india-s-cow-crisis-part-1-nepal-bears-the-brunt-of-india-s-cow-vigilantism-62703

Johari, A. 2017. Two Years after Maharashtra's Beef Ban, Mumbai's Qureshi Butcher Community Struggles with Poverty. *Scroll,* 2 April, https://scroll.in/article/833198/two-years-after-maharashtras-beef-ban-mumbais-qureshi-butcher-community-struggles-with-poverty

Karpagam S., and Joshi, S. 2021. Criminalizing Livelihoods, Legalising Vigilantism: The Adverse Impact of the Karnataka Prevention of Slaughter and Preservation of Cattle Act, 2020. report_impact_cattle_slaughter-ban_karnataka.pdf (wordpress.com)

Laliwala, S., Gurmat, S., and Dhawan, P. 2023. How Majoritarian Policies in UP & Maharashtra sent Meat Industries into Decline, Ended Thousands of Jobs. *Article 14,* 19 July, https://article-14.com/post/how-majoritarian-policies-in-up-maharashtra-sent-meat-industries-into-decline-ended-thousands-of-jobs-64b749d7913b2

Lerche, J. 2013. The Agrarian Question in Neoliberal India: Agrarian Transition Bypassed? *Journal of Agrarian Change* 13 (3): 382–404.

Lerche, J. 2021. The Farm Laws Struggle 2020–2021: Class-caste Alliances and Bypassed Agrarian Transition in Neoliberal India. *Journal of Peasant Studies* 48 (7): 1380–1396.

Mahapatra, R. 2012. Rise of Livestock. *Down to Earth,* 31 January, https://www.downtoearth.org.in/coverage/rise-of-livestock-35670

Mampatta, S., and Kant, K. 2018. Holy Cow! Now Even India Inc Spends Money on them. *Rediff,* 22 November, https://www.rediff.com/money/special/holy-cow-now-even-india-inc-spends-money-on-them/20181122.htm

Mander, H. 2023. Cows, Vigilantes and Meo Muslims in Nuh. *Caravan*, 3 August, https://caravanmagazine.in/politics/cows-vigilantes-and-meo-muslims-in-nuh-haryana

Matthan, T. 2022. Speculative Crops: Gambling on the Onion in India. *Geoforum* 130: 115–122.

Mishra, A. 2022. Stray Animals Destroy Crops in UP Districts as Goshalas Remain Non-Starters. *India Today,* 11 January, https://www.indiatoday.in/india/story/stray-animals-crops-up-districts-goshalas-non-starters-1898440-2022-01-10

Moudgil, M. 2017. UP's Slaughterhouse Crackdown: Butchers, Farmers, Traders Hit, Big Businesses Gain. *Indiaspend,* 15 July, https://www.indiaspend.com/ups-slaughterhouse-crackdown-butchers-farmers-traders-hit-big-businesses-gain-92135/

Moudgil, M. 2022. Five Years of UP's Animal Slaughter Ban: Poor Pushed Out of Meat Trade, Meat Out of Meals. *Janata Weekly,* 30 January, https://janataweekly.org/five-years-of-ups-animal-slaughter-ban-poor-pushed-out-of-meat-trade-meat-out-of-meals/

Münster, D. 2015. "Ginger Is a Gamble": Crop Booms, Rural Uncertainty, and the Neoliberalization of Agriculture in South India. *Focaal* 71: 100–113.

Narayanan, Y. 2018. Cow Protection as "Casteised Speciesism": Sacralisation, Commercialisation and Politicisation. *South Asia: Journal of South Asian Studies* 41 (2): 331–351.

Narayanan, Y. 2019. "Cow Is a Mother, Mothers Can Do Anything for Their Children!" Gaushalas as Landscapes of Anthropatriarchy and Hindu Patriarchy. *Hypatia* 34 (2): 195–221.

Narayanan, Y. 2023. *Mother Cow, Mother India: A Multispecies Politics of Dairy in India.* Stanford: Stanford University Press.

Nilsen, A. G. 2023. Feast, Famine, and Hegemony: On Neoliberalisation and Hindu Nationalism in India. *Polity,* https://ssalanka.org/feast-famine-and-hegemony-on-neoliberalisation-and-hindu-nationalism-in-india-alf-gunvald-nilsen/

Noronha, R. 2018. Till the Cows Come Home: Can Gaushalas Solve Farmers' Woes? *India Today,* 2 April, https://www.indiatoday.in/magazine/the-big-story/story/20180402-uttar-pradesh-yogi-adityanath-cow-shelter-budget-gaushalas-1196432-2018-03-22

OpIndia. 2021. Gaushala Scam in Rajasthan: Over 62 Lakh Worth of Government Grant Paid to Six Cow Shelters Without a Single Cow. 24 March, https://www.opindia.com/2021/03/gaushala-scam-rajasthan-62-lakh-worth-government-money-without-single-cow/
Patel, A. 2017. Holy Cow! Shocking State of Affairs in "Gaushalas" of Uttar Pradesh. *India Today*, 21 June, https://www.indiatoday.in/india/story/gau-shalas-uttar-pradesh-cow-shelters-maneka-gandhi-yogi-adityanath-969641-2017-04-05
Pattenden, J. (2016). *Labour, State and Society in Rural India: A Class-Relational Approach*. Manchester: Manchester University Press.
Pattenden, J. 2023. Progressive Politics and Populism: Classes of Labour and Rural–Urban Political Sociology – An Introduction to the Special Issue. *Journal of Agrarian Change* 23 (1): 3–21.
Ramdas, S. R. 2017a. The Beef Ban Effect: Stray Cattle, Broken Markets and Boom Time for Buffaloes. *The Wire*, 6 April, https://thewire.in/politics/beef-ban-cattle-market
Ramdas, S. R. 2017b. The Sordid Truth About the BJP's Drive Against Meat in UP. *The Wire*, 8 April, https://thewire.in/politics/up-illegal-meat-bjp
Ramdas, S. R. 2020a. Concentration of the Livestock Sector: Through the Lens of Milk and Meat. In *Corporate Concentration in Agriculture and Food*, edited by Premkumar, L., 29–43. N.p.: Focus on the Global South, Alternative Law Forum & Rosa Luxemburg Stiftung.
Ramdas, S. R. 2020b. Will Karnataka's New Bill Sound the Death Knell for Its Cattle Wealth? *The Leaflet*, 15 December, https://www.theleaflet.in/will-karnatakas-new-bill-sound-the-death-knell-for-its-cattle-wealth/#
Salve, P. 2020. "Cow Vigilantism Has Led to a Major Collapse in Animal Markets and Hurt Farm Incomes": Cattle Expert. *Scroll*, 12 March, https://scroll.in/article/955725/cow-vigilantism-has-led-to-a-major-collapse-in-animal-markets-and-hit-farm-incomes-cattle-expert
Shah, A., and Harriss-White, B. 2011. Resurrecting Scholarship on Agrarian Transformations. *Economic and Political Weekly* 46 (39): 13–18.
Sharma, A. 2017. Cows a Boon for Mankind, Says Yogi Adityanath Approving Gaushalas in Uttar Pradesh. *Economic Times*, 1 September, https://economictimes.indiatimes.com/news/politics-and-nation/cows-a-boon-for-mankind-says-yogi-adityanath-approving-gaushalas-in-uttar-pradesh/articleshow/60317695.cms?from=mdr
Shenoy, J. 2020. Centre to Provide Rs 900 Crore to Registered Gaushalas in India: Nirmala Sitharaman. *Times of India*, 11 November, https://timesofindia.indiatimes.com/business/india-business/centre-to-provide-rs-900-crore-to-registered-goshalas-in-india-nirmala-sitharaman/articleshow/79176296.cms
Siddiqui, Z., et al. 2017. Emboldened by Modi's Ascent, India's Cow Vigilantes Deny Muslims their Livelihoods. *Reuters*, 6 November, https://www.reuters.com/investigates/special-report/india-politics-religion-cows/
Singh, J. 2017. UP's Anti-abbatoir Campaign Could Cripple Prime Revenue – and Job-generating Industries. *Indiaspend*, 29 March, https://www.indiaspend.com/ups-anti-abattoir-campaign-could-cripple-prime-revenue-and-job-generating-industries-33121
Sood, A. R. 2022. "We're Finished": Farmers, Traders say Karnataka Cattle Slaughter Law Brought Years of Misery. *The Print*, 10 January, https://theprint.in/india/were-finished-farmers-traders-say-karnataka-cattle-slaughter-law-brought-year-of-misery/796924/
Staples, J. 2019. Blurring Bovine Boundaries: Cow Politics and the Everyday in South India. *South Asia: Journal of South Asian Studies* 42 (6): 1125–1140.

Staples, J. 2020. *Sacred Cows and Chicken Manchurian: The Everyday Politics of Eating Meat in India*. Seattle: University of Washington Press.
Sur, M. 2020. Time at Its Margins: Cattle Smuggling Across the India-Bangladesh Border. *Cultural Anthropology* 35 (4): 546–574.
Tayob, S. 2019. Disgust as Embodied Critique: Being Middle Class and Muslim in Mumbai. *South Asia: Journal of South Asian Studies* 42 (6): 1192–1209.
Tehelka. 2023. Cow Smuggling Files. 2 August, http://tehelka.com/cow-smuggling-files/
Vasavi, A. R. 2012. *Shadow Space: Suicides and the Predicament of Rural India*. Haryana: Three Essays Collective.

4 Towards Corporate Concentration
COVID-19 and Beyond

In 2020, Sagari Ramdas (2020: 40), a leading authority on India's bovine economy and politics, wrote that the attempts to disrupt the beef trade through legal and extra-legal means may in effect be "a sinister mechanism for the wealth in this trade to be captured by the organised industry". Not long ago, this organised industry was the world's largest exporter of beef by volume, with the value of beef exports touching almost USD 5 billion. Yet even this considerable figure pales when we take into account that somewhere between 60 and 80 percent of all buffalo meat being processed in India remains in the unorganised sector and is consumed domestically (*Processed Food Industry Online* 2020). The potential "wealth to be captured" referred to by Ramdas is, in other words, considerable.

Ramdas's proposition about the usurping advance of the organised industry was founded on the assumption that the neoliberal economic policies of the Modi regime that we described in previous chapters generally favours large corporates *and* produce corporate concentration across sectors. With most of India's "bovine wealth" located in the informal and unorganised sector, a disruption of this sector would, Ramdas suggests, potentially enable the organised industry to move in and capture the value generated there, significantly altering class and accumulation dynamics in the bovine economy. How, then, have things developed since Ramdas presented her hypothesis in 2020? Have developments proven her right, or have class and accumulation dynamics in the bovine economy reverted to "business as usual"?

We examine these questions in this chapter to show how the political moment of Modi's authoritarian populism and its legal and extra-legal crackdown on the beef trade has in fact set in motion a process that is already leading to broader sectoral restructurings of the kind that Ramdas predicted. These restructurings that are central to the economic moment of Modi's authoritarian populism, we suggest, may in the longer run further undermine important sectors in the informal economy in which most of India's classes of labour navigate, and lead to greater corporate concentration in beef-dependent sectors. To substantiate this argument, we proceed as follows. We start by outlining the initial impact on the organised beef industry of the shocks of

DOI: 10.4324/9781032709406-4

Hindu nationalist vigilante violence and legislative crackdowns. We then analyse the industry's subsequent recovery, before we discuss the impact of the COVID-19 pandemic on both the organised and unorganised industry. The differential impact of the pandemic and pandemic-related measures on these two sectors, the growing popularity of frozen food during and after COVID-19, and new and expansive forms of state support for dairy and meat production under the newly launched Atmanirbhar Bharat Mission which seeks to make India self-sufficient are all, we argue, drivers of changing class and accumulation dynamics that further corporate concentration and consolidation. In other words, we show how the bovine politics and economics of the Modi regime increasingly benefit politically favoured classes of corporate capital. When read alongside the previous chapter's argument that the incorporation of classes of labour in Modi's political project increasingly occurs through the destruction of key parts of their livelihoods, the state contradictions that this book is centrally concerned with are arguably moving towards being *less* contradictory insofar as the political and economic moments of Modi's authoritarian populism increasingly align in an intensifying manner.

Impact on the Organised Export-Oriented Industry

In light of the generalised targeting of the bovine economy described in previous chapters, it is not surprising to find that the organised and export-oriented industry was also initially negatively affected by the crackdown on the bovine economy. As figure 2.1 showed, meat exports declined quite sharply from 2014–2015 to 2015–2016, and more gradually from 2017–2018 to 2020–2021. While general supply chain disruptions through legal and extra-legal means are implicated in the early drop, the 2017 closure of slaughterhouses running without requisite permits in Uttar Pradesh – the hub of the export industry – played a key role in the latter decline at it significantly hit the large, export-oriented abattoirs located in that state (Jeelani 2017). In Uttar Pradesh, nine formally registered export units were closed by the authorities for some time, while a few other export facilities closed of their own volition for a time, to avoid controversy. This included companies such as Al Hamd Agro Foods and HMA Agro Industries, who shut down immediately after the state government began its campaign to close the slaughterhouses. But even those export units who were in possession of the required permits and licenses and remained in business suffered from the general disruption of supply chains and had to operate at heavily reduced capacity, sometimes as low as 20 to 25 percent. Faced with an urgent shortage of meat, industrial beef exporters struggled to capitalise on the economically important exports to countries in the Middle East during Ramadan, when exports double compared to other times of the year. In 2017, these exports were significantly delayed or cancelled altogether, causing a loss of goodwill, face, and money for Indian meat exporters (Fauzan Alavi cited in Kaushik 2017), while also raising concerns among exporters that Brazilian and Australian exporters would move in to capture lucrative markets in the Middle East. According to Allanasons, for example, the value of its meat exports dropped by a full USD 90 million in the month of March 2017 alone, compared to the same month the previous year (Kaushik 2017). The losses across the entire meat sector were estimated to be twice as much.

This may sound like the recipe for a generalised crisis also in the formal sector dominated by large, export-oriented actors running mechanised and well-equipped slaughterhouses, especially when one factors in that the organised meat industry in several states has been the target of various other forms of disruptive state intervention that have undermined its operational capacity – such as police investigations into allegations of exporters illegally exporting cow meat disguised as buffalo (Ohri 2018); or Income Tax department raids of offices, factories and residences, and the seizing of properties (Salaria 2022). And yet, trade data suggest that the export-oriented formal sector weathered the storm of cow vigilantism and other disruptive activities much better than did domestic, informal markets and actors. In Uttar Pradesh, for example, most large export-units were in fact in possession of the required permits. This meant that they could soon return to operations while the government slaughterhouses and the informal sector more generally descended into long-term stagnation and decline. This would, in turn, mean that the big private players in beef in Uttar Pradesh that were created as export points gradually began to make inroads also into domestic beef markets: With the municipal slaughterhouses closed, the main destination for cattle for slaughter and hence the main legal source of meat supply for small butchers selling meat was now the corporate slaughter houses of the organised industry (Laliwala, Gurmat, and Dhawan 2023a). As a result, small butchers gradually became vertically integrated into the export companies (Salve 2020) who thereby captured a part of the value generated in the informal domestic market.

The growing presence of the organised industry in the domestic market also signalled a small but important opening into the domestic market for frozen meat products that had hitherto largely been exported. In the domestic market, fresh or so-called "hot meat" traditionally dominates and is sold in unpacked form. Most people who purchase meat do so from local meat shops where small-scale butchers slaughter a few animals throughout the day, as per demand. This means that the time gap between slaughter and sale is very short, with most meat being slaughtered, sold, and consumed on the same day. There has in addition traditionally been a strong consumer preference for fresh over frozen meat, based on the belief that the latter is "not fresh" and lacking in taste and flavour compared to its fresh counterpart. As a result, the domestic retail market for frozen meat products has generally been small. Yet the sudden dearth of fresh meat in the market following the 2017 crackdown in Uttar Pradesh, however, created an opening for frozen meat also domestically, presenting frozen meat as an option for consumers, and effecting a slight but not insignificant market shift in favour of corporate producers of frozen meat products who operate at scale (Moudgil 2017). As we demonstrate later in the chapter, this development was further amplified during the COVID-19 pandemic.

Long-Term Sectoral Restructuring

While the early consequences of the crackdown on the beef trade was thus to throw the informal sector into an immediate crisis while simultaneously creating new market openings for corporate actors, recent reports from Uttar Pradesh from 2022 to 2023 bear out how these two trends have accelerated since 2017. A report from early 2022 by Manu Moudgil found that almost all government-run slaughterhouses in Uttar Pradesh had remained shut since 2017 – despite an order from the High Court in Allahabad in 2017 directing the government to upgrade and subsequently issue new licences to slaughterhouses who meet formal requirements. This prolonged closure of the state-run abattoirs has affected thousands of small-scale meat sellers who depended on these abattoirs for their business. Prior to the closure of the government slaughterhouses, for example, 80 out of the approximately 100 buffaloes that were slaughtered in the city of Kanpur every day would be slaughtered at these facilities. Here, meat sellers and vendors who lacked adequate slaughter facilities of their own (the case for the vast majority) could bring an animal, pay a fee of INR 25, and then take away the meat and other animal parts for resale. It was also possible for small vendors without the means to afford a whole buffalo to buy smaller portions of meat for resale from government slaughterhouses (Moudgil 2022). The long-term closure of the slaughterhouses has meant that many small vendors have quit the trade for good. Compounding this critical situation, animal rearers in rural Uttar Pradesh finding livestock prices on the decline alongside rising fodder costs have been forced to reduce their flocks. As a result, according to one meat retailer, no more than 5 percent of the state's butchers and meat dealers were in business by 2022. The rest, he argued, had moved to selling vegetables, plying rickshaws, or dealing in junk (Moudgil 2022).

Other reports from Uttar Pradesh confirm Moudgil's findings, noting that many small butchers and meat traders have lost their jobs for want of supply, or because of a fear-induced drop in demand. And, those who remained in business were further squeezed by a set of requirements for the meat sector, in effect since 2017, which operate with so constricting, complicated and specific requirements that no small shops had the infrastructure or manpower to implement them (Dev 2017). Anecdotal estimates from butchers in Uttar Pradesh in 2023 suggest that while profits have dropped, fees and bribes have risen tenfold as small butchers and traders increasingly have to pay the relevant authorities to turn a blind eye (Laliwala, Gurmat, and Dhawan 2023a). In addition, fear looms large among both customers and butchers about further crackdowns, including everyday forms of vigilantism (Deepak 2023).

In contrast, the organised industry has in several ways benefited from the state-engineered crisis in the informal sector. In the city of Kanpur, the Kanpur Municipal Corporation after some time started issuing licenses to smaller meat retailers to once again operate in the city. The condition, however, was that they procure their meat from the modern slaughterhouses run by private companies that were previously export-only operations. Hence, these companies are moving into and consolidating their position in the domestic market too, enabled by the local municipal corporation. With local retailers having to purchase from these units, meat prices reportedly rose to become the highest in the state, while shopkeepers' profit margins simultaneously waned. As one Kanpur retailer complained: "Most retailers buying meat from export houses are under debt because their profit margin has reduced". Simultaneously, whereas the small retailers used to get horns, hide, fat (tallow) and other materials that are all tradeable items that brought small profits when they procured meat from government slaughterhouses, the large units retain these items, thereby depriving small traders of a small but important source of income. Independent medium intermediary traders who earlier supplied meat to several shops or supermarkets have also been pushed out of the business for want of licenses and permits and have witnessed large frozen meat companies moving in to take over their clients (Laliwala, Gurmat, and Dhawan 2023a; Moudgil 2022).

Small retailers elsewhere in Uttar Pradesh have fared no better. In the important city of Lucknow, for example, not a single butcher or meat seller has been issued a no-objection certificate or licence to operate. Whatever remains of the informal business has been driven underground, resulting in lower profit margins for butchers and traders, who now live under "a cloud of uncertainty and fear of an official crackdown" (Moudgil 2022). In smaller towns and villages, the forced closure of slaughterhouses and meat shops has, effectively, finished off these businesses entirely. While many have therefore left the meat business, some former retailers who can no longer legally slaughter and sell meat, have shifted to selling live buffaloes to the large export houses instead. But, compared to buying and butchering a buffalo, and selling its meat and various other products, the selling of live buffaloes generates much lower incomes. Evidently, then, a key effect of the unfolding dynamics of Hindu nationalist bovine politics has indeed been that much of the wealth that was earlier produced and retained in the informal bovine economy among classes of labour in city and countryside has now been captured by the organised industry.

We see comparable forms of corporate concentration evolving also in related sectors. In contrast to the collapse of the Pechbagh hide market in Uttar Pradesh that we described in the previous chapter, and which depended largely on supplies from municipal slaughterhouses and rural classes of labour, the big tanneries and exporters remained in business. Tellingly, these can source hides widely, obtaining them directly from the large, mechanised privately run slaughterhouses, or even from abroad. Reports from Uttar Pradesh from 2023 additionally suggest that a significant chunk of activities previously carried out by traders, middle-men and labourers involved in obtaining, transporting, and salting raw hides has now been taken over by the large corporate slaughterhouses that do the salting and tanning themselves, and sell the hides directly to leather manufacturers (Laliwala, Gurmat, and Dhawan 2023b).

Similarly, the handicraft sector has witnessed comparable forms of restructuring. Take artisans in the district town of Sambhal in western Uttar Pradesh, for example, known for its handicrafts made from animal bones and horns. With the collapse of the informal market, local suppliers of these raw materials were forced out of market, and artisans have shifted to buying bones and horns from the meat-exporting units. Tellingly, both items are now considerably more expensive than earlier, and profit margins slimmer (Moudgil 2022). Such stronger linkages between large capitalists operating in the slaughter and post-slaughter economies of meat, leather, and handicraft arguably index greater corporate concentration across multiple sectors of the bovine economy.

Beef Exports Bounce Back

Another indicator of the organised industry doing well when compared to the prolonged crisis in the informal, domestic sector, can be found in export statistics. If we examine the post-2016 period, we find that 2017–2018 was all in all a good year for Indian beef exporters. A significant decline measured in metric tonnes carcass weight equivalent only set in in 2018 and, more dramatically, around 2020. While the drop in exports for 2018 is arguably connected to the crackdown on the trade in beef and therefore documents the hit that this sector also took, the drop in 2020 had more to do with the COVID-19 pandemic. During India's early and extremely strict lockdown from March 2020 onwards (Nilsen 2022), many meat export-processing units had to close partially or wholly for several months. The essential long supply chains stretching from classes of labour in the countryside to urban slaughterhouses were broken, and while the shorter supply chains near urban centres remained mostly functional, the overall result was nonetheless a pandemically induced virtual "collapse" of the meat trade (Sarkar 2020). Whereas India's beef export industry would in an average month export more than 100,000 tonnes of buffalo meat, exports in March 2020 when the lockdown was imposed stood at only 40,000 tonnes. In April it was even less (Chu and Jadhav 2020). This form of partial collapse is not unique to India, and similar patterns have been noted for global meat production and supply chains under COVID-19 more generally (Ijaz et al. 2021).

Post-pandemic beef exports continued to remain at a lower level than before the pandemic as the industry's recovery after the strict first lockdown was further hampered by another COVID-19 related factor: In 2021 during the second wave of the pandemic that swept India with devastating effect (Nilsen forthcoming), several countries imposed temporary bans on imports of Indian beef citing COVID-19 concerns. This included Indonesia and Cambodia. Yet despite such bans, overall beef exports from India in 2021 nonetheless increased somewhat compared to the year before because beef production was picking up in states with large water buffalo populations, especially Uttar Pradesh, Maharashtra, and Andhra Pradesh (FAS/USDA 2023), enabled by local livestock markets that were gradually reopening. This recovery is arguably at least in part the outcome of significant backing for the industry from the Modi regime. Unlike during the first lockdown in 2020, the government in 2021 saw to it that the dairy and meat industries were unaffected by lockdown measures, ensuring the unhindered inter/intra-state movement of animals to slaughterhouses and processing facilities (Mani et al. 2021). This enabled the export industry to "operate as normally as possible", despite the pandemic. Such state support translates into higher export figures which have climbed after 2020 to almost reach 2018–2019 levels, even if the picture is not quite as positive in terms of value. The export industry's ability to bounce back from multiple setbacks and complications becomes even more significant in light of the fact that Indian beef exports to Vietnam have declined dramatically in only a few years. As we noted earlier, Vietnam used to be the number one destination for Indian beef, accounting for more than half of India's exported beef in 2017–2018. By 2020–2021, this had dropped to merely 11 percent in volume terms and 13 percent by value. What is notable is that this fall in exports to Vietnam has been successfully offset by an almost equally large increase in exports to other destinations, especially Egypt and Indonesia (*Euromeatnews* 2022), with the Indian government currently working to add Bangladesh to the list of importing countries (Mahmud 2022).

Recent developments in trade with countries in the Middle East, and the Gulf in particular, also have important implications for beef exports. An emerging "India-Middle East Food Corridor" linking India to Israel and the United Arab Emirates (UAE) is underway. According to a recent analysis, the corridor "originated in the symbiosis between the Arab Gulf states' strategic need to ensure their food security and India's strategic imperative to increase the value of its food production" (Tunchum 2022). While the UAE had already laid plans for massive investments in food processing facilities through the private sector in various Indian cities back in 2017, the corridor was triggered further by increased recognition of vulnerabilities in supply chains from

COVID-19 as well as Ukraine war shocks (*Gulf News* 2022). The UAE has emerged as India's third foremost trade partner, with the UAE heavily reliant on imports of food items – including buffalo meat – from India (Paliwal 2022). In the post-COVID period, Modi has put significant diplomatic efforts into relations with the UAE, including visits and apologies following anti-Muslim controversies in India (AP News 2022), the signing of a massive free-trade agreement (Sharma 2022), and the ongoing construction of UAE's first traditional stone Hindu temple (Kumar 2023). The significant political work thus invested in strengthening trade ties between India and the Middle East is likely to also benefit India's beef export industry.

Export-oriented production has thus recovered relatively quickly and efficiently from the multiple disruptions of the business, and certainly quicker than domestically oriented production and trade. Indeed, recent reports from the important states of Maharashtra and Uttar Pradesh speak of significantly declining local consumption and sale of beef meat amidst high levels of activity at the slaughterhouses and rising expert revenues from beef (Laliwala, Gurmat, and Dhawan 2023b) – clear indications of a thriving export sector. There has also been talk of the decline in domestic consumption in the year 2020 being triggered by the "strong demand for export carabeef [that] kept local supply tight" (FAS/USDA 2023). In 2022, the prospects for the meat industry as a whole were spoken of as good. According to a March 2022 forecast by the USDA, India's total cattle slaughter was expected to increase by close to 2 million heads compared to the year before, and by nearly 5 million heads compared to the disastrous year 2020 (Mani et al. 2021). Domestic consumer demand for beef was also reported to once again be "strong", with the domestic consumption of beef expected to increase by 130,000 MT carcass weight equivalent compared to 2021. For export production, however, predictions were even better, with an estimated increase in production of a full 150,000 MT carcass weight equivalent. These prognoses were somewhat rattled by the sudden outbreak of a cattle disease known as "lumpy skin disease", which hit the country in late 2022. It affected 2.4 million animals and killed over 110,000 cattle within a period of some weeks only, with Rajasthan and Maharashtra the most severely hit (Arora 2022). This also affected exports which – as Figure 2.1 shows – increased by a good deal less than the anticipated 150,000 MT carcass weight equivalent. In 2023, beef exports also experienced a certain slowdown due to the Egyptian currency crisis – Egypt, as we have seen, recently assuming a central position among key importers of Indian beef (*Moneycontrol* n.d.b). Yet if the statistics for April to June 2023 can be taken as indicative of the year as a whole, total exports for 2023 should see no decline compared to the year before – it might even see a modest increase. What we find is thus a strong and expansive recovery in the corporate-controlled export sector unfolding alongside a reasonably good but uneven and delayed recovery also in domestic beef production – with the significant difference compared to a decade ago that the organised industry now plays a bigger role in and captures an increased share of the wealth of that sector.

Pandemic Developments: Frozen Food and Self-Reliance

While some Hindu nationalist groups sought to further their political agenda at the expense of the meat industry by stoking rumours that COVID-19 spread exclusively via non-vegetarian food (Fischer 2023: 1), the COVID-19 pandemic was in several respects not entirely bad news for the beef export industry and the corporate food sector more generally. Two important developments during the pandemic in particular have further boosted corporate concentration in these sectors: The growing prevalence of frozen foods in urban diets; and the increasing emphasis on self-reliance in central government policy. Below we discuss these two developments and outline how they contribute to growing corporate concentration and the shaping of new class and accumulation dynamics.

The Rise of Frozen Food and Meat

As discussed above, the presence of frozen or even processed meat in domestic diets is a relatively new phenomenon as most consumers prefer their meat to be fresh, slaughtered on the same day as it is to be cooked and consumed at home. A survey of consumers' attitudes towards meat consumption in Delhi and Hyderabad conducted as recently as 2016 (Suresh 2016) found that most meat consumers had in fact never purchased neither packaged meat products nor processed meat items. However, frozen food has been gaining in social acceptability and popularity for some years now, for a variety of reasons having to do with convenience, year-round availability, popularity among younger consumers and "working couples", and easy availability in urban areas. Market expansion in frozen food has been enabled by the expansion of modern retail outlets with cooling facilities. Urban India in particular has undergone a retail revolution within the last few years, with new "hypermarkets" mushrooming in urban spaces, where a variety of frozen (and fresh) meat and fish are sold alongside vegetarian products "on a massive scale under one roof" (Fischer 2023: 14). As described by Fischer (2023: 73) from Hyderabad, these hypermarkets are often "designed to accommodate the sale of meat/fish", with elaborate procedures in place for handling and storing both, including cold rooms and ice makers. Moreover, eating meat that has been purchased in such sanitised shopping spaces is increasingly being promoted as a healthy and nutritious option. In addition to the proliferation of hypermarkets, the growth in online retail sales that was further accelerated by the COVID-19 pandemic has opened up another avenue for the purchase of frozen meat and other frozen foods. Online retail shopping is perceived as a sector with tremendous growth potential over the next few years, with one report suggesting that upwards of 400 million Indians will be shopping online, spending USD 140 to 160 billion annually, already by 2025 (Roy 2023).

In tandem with these retail and online revolutions, the range of frozen foods that are available has grown tremendously within a short amount of time. From a situation where frozen products were limited to green peas, nuggets, French fries, and a few others, today's frozen food market includes a vast range of snacks, fruits, vegetables, and dairy and meat products. The Indian frozen foods market is predicted to grow rapidly during the years ahead, with the estimated market worth increasing from INR 42.7 billion in 2021 to INR 93.8 billion in 2025 – a full 17 percent per year (Yadav 2022). Chain restaurants remain a key driver of this market, whereas the retail market accounts for around one third of the total frozen foods market (Jamsudkar 2022). Within this bigger picture, the domestic consumption of frozen meat and seafood is still small but growing at a rate of 10 percent per year (Jamsudkar 2022).

The COVID-19 pandemic and the strict lockdown imposed in India have further increased the acceptability and popularity of frozen food. Fearing viral exposure, many people chose to stock up on frozen rather than fresh food to minimise the number of trips made to the store. Frozen food was also available through e-commerce sites, enabling consumers to make bulk purchases without going out. According to a spokesperson of the online grocery firm Grofers, categories like packaged foods – that is, food that is ready to eat and ready to cook – grew by up to 80 percent, while sales of frozen foods went up by as much as 500 percent from February to April 2020 (*Moneycontrol* n.d.). For 2020 as a whole, the growth rate of frozen foods was more than 20 percent, compared to 10 percent for fresh food sales (Yadav 2022). This arguably makes the market for frozen food one of the best performing sectors in an Indian economy that otherwise plunged during the pandemic.

The rise in the popularity of frozen foods and meat during and after the pandemic is also reflected in the increase in sales of deep freezers, which reportedly doubled in the span of just three years, from the summer of 2019 to the summer of 2022 (Jamsudkar 2022). As we know from decades of consumption research, technologies such as refrigerators and deep freezers are not just indicative of, but also *generative* of new food practices and habits. The introduction of refrigerators and deep freezers into private homes requires an extensive surrounding infrastructure, including refrigerated warehouses for wholesale storage, refrigerated transport, and refrigerated sections of retail food stores (Wilhite 2016: 52–58). Such infrastructure and systems of provision is increasingly in place in major Indian metropolises (Fischer 2023), making home-owned deep freezers a meaningful purchase for those who can afford one. Refrigerators and deep freezers enable the storage of frozen, chilled and ready-made meals, as well as bulk purchases of food, whether in person or through online shops (Wilhite 2016: 52–58). As research from Western Europe and North America shows, these new possibilities radically alter food practices that increasingly become centred precisely on ready-made and frozen foods. Importantly, in these contexts, refrigeration and freezing have been central to the growth in meat consumption over the past half century. As one study shows, from the time when refrigerators became standard home appliances in the USA in the 1950s up until 2010, annual meat consumption increased by five times.

Although there is currently little research on the impact of domestic deep freezers on Indian food practices, Wilhite's (2008) study of the introduction of refrigerators into private homes in the state of Kerala suggests that developments in India may likely follow a trajectory similar to that experienced in the global north. Refrigerators are, Wilhite shows, powerful change agents that affect both eating and food practices, altering the ways in which people think about food preparation, storage, and consumption. In the Kerala context, the acquisition of refrigerators led many young women to routinely make food in bulk, storing uneaten portions for later meals. As refrigeration and storing meals became routine aspects of food preparation, earlier ideologies that connected stored food to laziness and bad health gradually dissolved. Deep freezers arguably have a comparable potential to alter consumer perceptions about frozen food and meat, particularly in an Indian context where the corporate food industry is currently heavily invested in promoting frozen food, including meat, as healthier and safer to eat than its "fresh" counterparts. The fact that celebrity chefs have also endorsed frozen meat products (N. Sharma 2020) has added to their growing acceptability among upper class consumers. Important for the present discussion, however, is that the frozen food market is highly consolidated with just a few companies dominating the market. In the meat sector, this currently includes Venky's (poultry), Al Kabeer (meat), Innovative Foods (veg and non-veg), and a few others. Entry barriers are high as cold chain technology and end-to-end refrigeration solutions are expensive, up front capital investments high, and food and safety regulations strict (Jamsudkar 2022). As the market for frozen food and meat continues to expand, it is thus likely to remain concentrated in the hands of a small number of large corporate actors.

Atmanirbhar Bharat: Towards a Self-Reliant India

A related and no less relevant pandemically induced development is the growing emphasis on self-reliance in central government policy, including in the domains of agriculture and food production. While featuring in Modi's vocabulary for the entire period of his reign, it was as part of the pandemic response and associated economic contraction in 2020 that *Atmanirbhar Bharat* emerged as a popularised term for Modi's portfolio of ambitious and purportedly transformative programmes, "mentioned in virtually every speech made by Modi and his Cabinet, and made a key part of every legislative effort" (Joshi et al. 2021). Roughly translating into "self-reliant India", the term is seemingly applied to more or less anything the Modi government is doing, yet it adds a certain historical flair in its relatively explicitly articulated connotations to Gandhian ideas of *swaraj* and *swadeshi*, and India's struggle for independence (see, e.g. The Hindu 2022). As a 2020 report on Modi's initiative held, it has a distinctly contradictory look – appearing, on the surface, as rather *un*-neoliberal – raising certain concerns in the world of business, as "Modi's policy aims to reduce domestic market access to imports, but at the same time open the economy and export to the rest of the world" (S. Sharma 2020).

Food and agriculture arise – unsurprisingly – as central concerns in this recent rhetoric of a "self-reliant" India. As part of the Atmanirbhar Bharat branded COVID-19 response announced by the central government in 2020 was a central attention to livestock in the establishment of a new Animal Husbandry Infrastructure Development Fund (AHIDF) of INR 15,000 crore. This fund aims at incentivising investments in the dairy sector in particular, including upgrading of infrastructure, as well as meat processing, to generate economic growth and increased exports from livestock. Explicitly seeking enhanced private sector investments, there is little doubt about the pro-corporate design of the AHIDF, which also was preceded in 2018 by an ambitious new agricultural export policy seeking to double agro-food export by 2022. "High-value" produce, including meat, is emphasised in both the fund and the export policy as well as in statements by leading agricultural economists in the country. In April 2023, the central government announced that the AHIDF would be merged with another fund in existence from the early 2000s, the Dairy Processing and Infrastructure Development Fund, "with the goal of allocating funds from the balance outlay to private-sector dairy and meat processing units" (Saxena 2023). According to the 2022–2023 Economic Survey, the livestock sector is already witnessing noticeable growth:

> The livestock sector grew at a CAGR of 7.9 per cent during 2014–15 to 2020–21 (at constant prices), and its contribution to total agriculture GVA (at constant prices) has increased from 24.3 per cent in 2014–15 to 30.1 per cent in 2020–21.
>
> (Press Information Bureau Delhi 2023)

Recent developments in Karnataka exemplify the pro-corporate design, and class-specific accumulation dynamics, of these ongoing restructurings of the livestock sector. In late 2022, the BJP Home Minister Amit Shah announced "cooperation" to be instilled between the Karnataka Cooperative Milk Federation (KMF) and Gujarat's Anand Milk Union Limited (Amul) aiming at the establishment of a nation-wide system to serve as the "export house" for planned entries in milk markets in neighbouring countries. Following analysis by the activist-journalist Shivasundar (2023), this move can be interpreted as part of a concerted effort by the central government of taking control over independent cooperatives. Central agricultural policymakers in the NITI Aayog, Shivasundar writes, have formulated intentions of "corporatising" existing cooperatives and deregulating the sector for private investments towards strengthening export. In a similar vein, Ramdas argues for seeing these developments as attempts at vertically integrating hitherto informal production into dairy agribusiness (Ramdas 2021).

While the upgrading of meat processing facilities aiming for enhanced export is explicitly part of these initiatives, it appears from Modi's speeches on the topic that his main interest in the livestock sector is in dairy. Praising the efforts of "small farmers" in making India into the world's largest milk producer, Modi's rhetorical invocation of postcolonial India's longer history of "milk nationalism" (Narayanan 2023) weaves dairy cattle into his vision of nationalist productivism. While dairy, not meat, thus appears as the central concern in Atmanirbhar Bharat, we know that the two are inseparable in workings of the agrarian political economy of livestock in India insofar as any increase in dairy production is certain to lead to a corresponding increase in the increasingly industrial slaughter of bovines (Narayanan 2023) and the export of beef meat to global markets. That beef and meat more generally therefore remain important for the current economic moment of the Modi regime, with its broader and ongoing restructurings supporting class-specific accumulation dynamics, is evident from the introduction, in June 2023, of the Livestock and Livestock Products (Importation and Exportation) Bill, 2023. Compared to the older law that this bill was intended to replace, it explicitly included bovines in its definition of livestock, and contained a new section on pro-actively promoting and developing the exports of livestock and livestock products from India, including fresh, chilled, and frozen meat and meat products of all kinds, as well as tissue and organs of bovines (Ramdas 2023).

Corporate Sector Alignment and Narratives of Waste and Value

Although the Livestock and Livestock Products (Importation and Exportation) Bill, 2023, was withdrawn before being passed into law – not least because (and unsurprisingly in view of the central state contradiction at work) it faced opposition from other sections of the wider Hindu nationalist movement, including the RSS, the Bharatiya Kisan Sangh, and various cow vigilante groups – the corporate meat sector has responded very positively to the many policy initiatives by the Modi government and have considerably aligned their public rhetoric accordingly.

An illustrative example of this can be found in an op-ed from late 2020, penned for CNBC-TV18 by Fauzan Alavi, the Spokesperson for the All-India Meat & Livestock Exporters Association and the Director of Allanasons. At this moment in time, Alavi could reasonably have complained about the damage done to his industry over several years by state-supported vigilantism, ever-tougher legislative restrictions, and various other forms of governmental crackdown. And, he could have encouraged the Modi government to change policy direction and curb the excesses of the vigilantes, citing the damage done to the national economy. But his op-ed made no references to this targeting of the bovine economy whatsoever. Instead, he addressed the state government of Uttar Pradesh, encouraging it to step up and lead India in buffalo meat exports. As India's largest beef exporting state by far, and as a state with no "social taboo on buffalo meat", Uttar Pradesh was in his view ideally positioned to do so, provided that it focused on modern and up-scaled abattoirs, logistics, and cold chain development. He also pointed to the great potential in frozen meats, ready-to-eat and semi-finished products that, as indicated above, have emerged as a new market for the corporate sector. This he, in turn, linked to Modi's Atmanirbhar Bharat mission: "To drive conditions for a bright future and boost economic growth, Prime Minister's Atma Nirbhar Bharat Abhiyaan stimulus package of Rs 15,000 crore for the Animal Husbandry Infrastructure Development Fund (AHIDF) exemplifies just that", he added. More specifically, Alavi zoomed in on the AHIDF's promise to increase India's meat processing capacity, the move towards an organised meat market, the emphasis on promoting the export contribution of the meat sector, and the expectation of establishing new meat processing units, upgrading value-added products, and facilitating the large-scale integration of meat processing facilities across the rural-urban divide. Also in line with AHIDF guidelines, Alavi stressed how "using spent animals leading to sustainable livestock development, developing secondary industries and livelihood opportunities, and creating wealth from waste" should become a mantra for India's states, and especially for Uttar Pradesh. This, he added, would also aid in fulfilling Modi's promises of doubling farmers' incomes and boosting India's exports of hides and finished leather products (Alavi 2020).

It is far from inconceivable that such rhetorical endorsement of key policies of the Modi government by the leading spokesperson of the corporate meat industry arises from well-grounded sentiments of fear. Indeed, a Muslim spokesperson for an industry often alleged to illegally be killing cows in the thousands criticising the policies of a well-entrenched Hindu nationalist government may all too easily have invited harsh retributions. Yet irrespective of the many motivations and considerations underlying Alavi's op-ed, it arguably goes a very long way in strategically aligning the interests and priorities of an industry that has otherwise often been – as our analysis of state contradictions in earlier chapters show – in a conflictual relationship with Hindu nationalism, with those of Modi's central government. What is equally noteworthy is Alavi's invocation of the trope of "waste to wealth" and his emphasis on the capacity of the organised and properly modernised and integrated industry to generate value from waste. This trope of "waste to value" is echoed in several writings by other representatives of the frozen meat or frozen food sector, a number of whom have been active in writing about their industries in the media and online fora the last years. In these writings, the unorganised meat industry is routinely portrayed as suffering from lack of proper surveillance, no veterinary control, inadequate amenities and facilities, and unhygienic conditions for both slaughter and retail trade, enhancing the risk of meat borne diseases and endangering the health and wellbeing of ordinary Indians. The ensuing call for prioritising the formal sector over the informal one that follows from this portrayal resonates well with "neoliberal demands for aesthetics, safety, health and hygiene" (Ahmad 2013: 121), to be achieved through modernisation, mechanisation, and economies of scale, and the elimination of the unclean and unsightly aspects of the informal meat industry. Additionally, the unorganised and informal meat sector is portrayed as a wasteful sector where good meat is spoilt, and related products under-utilised – a sector incapable of effectively utilising livestock resources to generate added value. To overcome this, and in striking contrast to Modi's scathing attack on India's "pink revolution" a decade ago, several authors from within the organised meat sector now occasionally call for a new "red revolution" in meat production (Suwal 2019; Yadav et al. 2020), to be driven by the organised, formal industry. Such a revolution would, as we know from, for example, Zarin Ahmad's (2013) study of the mechanisation and modernisation of slaughterhouses in Delhi from a decade ago, arguably unfold to the detriment of classes of labour in both city and countryside.

Conclusion

In this chapter, we have analysed a series of developments that have unfolded immediately prior to, during, and after the COVID-19 pandemic. While several of these developments – such as the crackdown on beef slaughter in Uttar Pradesh, and the strict pandemic lockdown – initially had a debilitating and disruptive effect also on the organised and export-oriented beef sector, these were relatively short-lived and relatively milder than what the informal sector was exposed to. Rather, the broader picture that emerges from our analysis is one of considerable corporate concentration across the bovine economy in the pandemic and post-pandemic period, facilitated by support from Modi's state and further aided by the neglect and even wilful destruction of the wider informal bovine economy.

In this regard, this chapter has provided further evidence to substantiate Ramdas' proposition that we began this chapter with, namely that the state-driven disruption of the informal beef trade under Modi as analysed across this book has, in practice, functioned as one important mechanism for the wealth in this trade to be captured by the organised industry. Another no less important mechanism driving this process has been, as this chapter has shown, active state support for the export-oriented large-scale beef sector organised around dominant class interests. In combination, these two mechanisms and the developments they have propelled have substantially altered class and accumulation dynamics across the bovine economy to the benefit of corporate and dominant class interests.

While we thus began this book with delving at length into the tenuous and strained relationship between state and capital in Modi's India as this manifested in the domain of bovine political economy, and into the contradiction between the political and economic moments of Modi's authoritarian populism that we have conceptualised as a state contradiction, the analysis in this chapter would suggest that we may currently be moving towards a scenario that is somewhat less contradictory (and where the bovine paradox is less paradoxical). This is a scenario where, as the example of India's bovine politics and economics has shown, the political and economic moments of Modi's authoritarian populism can increasingly be seen to align in an intensifying manner – albeit far from unproblematically – to restructure the Indian state and economy around dominant class interests, exemplified in this book through the progressive strengthening of the beef agro-industry and its class fractions, at the expense of rural and urban classes of labour in the informal economy. This compounds the difficulties the latter are already facing from the double victimisation described earlier, amounting to a veritable destruction of livelihoods. In the concluding chapter that follows, we reflect on the implications of this for the future of Modi's authoritarian populism, and for the possibility for progressive counter-hegemonic mobilisation.

References

Ahmad, Z. 2013. Marginal Occupations and Modernising Cities: Muslim Butchers in Urban India. *Economic and Political Weekly* 48 (32): 121–131.

Alavi, F. 2020. Explained: Here's How Uttar Pradesh Can Lead India in Buffalo Meat Exports. *CNBCTV*, 20 December, https://www.cnbctv18.com/india/explained-hereshow-uttar-pradesh-can-lead-india-in-buffalo-meat-exports-7836961.htm

AP News. 2022. India's Prime Minister Visits the UAE, Showcasing Deep Ties. 28 June, https://apnews.com/article/politics-india-dubai-united-arab-emirates-0320f976e6bbbacc37124dbd285114a4

Arora, M. 2022. Lumpy Skin Disease: Viral Cattle Disease Sends Rumours Flying in India. *BBC News,* 21 October, https://www.bbc.com/news/world-asia-india-63262411

Chu, M. M., and Jadhav, R. 2020. India's Coronavirus Lockdown Curbs Buffalo Meat Exports, Hitting Ramadan Supplies. *Reuters,* 3 May, https://www.reuters.com/article/ushealth-coronavirus-asia-beef-idUSKBN22F001

Deepak, S. 2023. India's Beef with Beef. *The Baffler* 67, https://thebaffler.com/salvos/indias-beef-with-beef-deepak

Dev, A. 2017. UP Lays Down Strict Guidelines for Meat Business. *Times of India,* 1 April, https://timesofindia.indiatimes.com/india/up-lays-down-strict-guidelines-for-meat-business/articleshow/57964695.cms

Euromeatnews. 2022. Vietnam's Low Demand for Beef Crashes the Indian Industry. 7 July, https://www.euromeatnews.com/Article-Vietnams-low-demand-for-beef-crashes-the-Indian-industry/4795

FAS/USDA. 2023. India Beef and Cattle Outlook. *Beef2live,* 19 June, https://beef2live.com/story-india-beef-cattle-outlook-0-142839

Fischer, J. 2023. *Vegetarianism, Meat and Modernity in India.* London: Routledge.

Gulf News. 2022. UAE Firms to Invest Up to $7 Billion in India-UAE Food Corridor: Indian Minister. 24 September, https://gulfnews.com/world/asia/india/uae-firms-to-invest-up-to-7-billion-in-india-uae-food-corridor-indian-minister-1.1569344178374

Ijaz, M., et al. 2021. Meat Production and Supply Chain Under COVID-19 Scenario: Current Trends and Future Prospects. *Frontiers in Veterinary Science* 8: article 660736.

Jamsudkar, M. 2022. Frozen Foods Take on Cool Factor. *Nuffoodsspectrum,* 31 July, https://nuffoodsspectrum.in/2022/07/31/frozen-foods-take-on-cool-factor.html

Jeelani, G. 2017. Job Loss Fear Looms Large over UP's Biggest Slaughtehouse where Hindus Outnumber Muslims. *Hindustan Times,* 3 April, https://www.hindustantimes.com/india-news/job-loss-fear-looms-over-up-s-biggest-slaughterhouse-where-hindus-outnumber-muslims/story-wodpKHLYmScJsJdsZZnjyO.html

Joshi, S. et al. 2021. "Atman Nirbhar Bharat" - Economic Crises and Self-reliance in the Covid-19 Pandemic. https://web.archive.org/web/20210308183606/https:/www.iaforum.org/Files/Atman%20Nirbhar%20Bharat_%20-%20Economic%20Crises%20and%20Self-Reliance%20in%20the%20COVID-19%20Pandemic.pdf

Kaushik, N. 2017. India's Beef Exports Hit by Cow Vigilantism. *Gulf News,* 17 May, https://gulfnews.com/lifestyle/indias-beef-exports-hit-by-cow-vigilantism-1.2028673

Kumar, A. 2023. Abu Dhabi Hindu Temple: Indian PM Modi Discusses Progress of UAE's First Traditional Stone Temple. *Khaleej Times,* 4 March, https://www.khaleejtimes.com/uae/abu-dhabi-hindu-temple-indian-pm-modi-discusses-progress-of-uaes-first-traditional-stone-temple

Laliwala, S., Gurmat, S., and Dhawan, P. 2023a. How Majoritarian Policies in UP & Maharashtra sent Meat Industries into Decline, Ended Thousands of Jobs. *Article 14,* 19 July, https://article-14.com/post/how-majoritarian-policies-in-up-maharashtra-sent-meat-industries-into-decline-ended-thousands-of-jobs-64b749d7913b2

Laliwala, S., Gurmat, S., and Dhawan, P. 2023b. Anti-Pollution Norms and State Policies Cripple UP's Leather Industries, Pushing Muslims Livelihoods to the Brink. *Article 14,* 21 July, https://article-14.com/post/anti-pollution-norms-state-policies-cripple-up-s-leather-industry-pushing-muslim-livelihoods-to-the-brink--64b9ed725f942?s=09

Mahmud, I. 2022. India Keen to Export Buffalo Meat to Bangladesh. *Prothom Alo,* 27 July, https://en.prothomalo.com/business/local/h60lr42v6b

Mani, R., et al. 2021. *Livestock and Products Semi-Annual 2022.* Washington, DC: United States Department of Agriculture, Foreign Agricultural Service.

Moneycontrol. n.d. Ready to Eat Foods See Huge Uptake Amid Second COVID-19 Surge in India. https://www.moneycontrol.com/europe/?url=https://www.moneycontrol.com/news/business/startup/ready-to-eat-foods-see-huge-uptake-amid-second-covid-19-surge-in-india-6862071.html

Moudgil, M. 2017. UP's Slaughterhouse Crackdown: Butchers, Farmers, Traders Hit, Big Businesses Gain. *Indiaspend,* 15 July, https://archive.indiaspend.com/cover-story/ups-slaughterhouse-crackdown-butchers-farmers-traders-hit-big-businesses-gain-92135

Moudgil, M. 2022. Five Years of UP's Animal Slaughter Ban: Poor Pushed Out of Meat Trade, Meat Out of Meals. *Janata Weekly,* 30 January, https://janataweekly.org/five-years-of-ups-animal-slaughter-ban-poor-pushed-out-of-meat-trade-meat-out-of-meals/

Narayanan, Y. 2023. *Mother Cow, Mother India: A Multispecies Politics of Dairy in India.* Stanford, CA: Stanford University Press.

Nilsen, A. G. 2022. India's Pandemic: Spectacle, Social Murder and Authoritarian Politics in a Lockdown Nation. *Globalizations* 19 (3): 466–486.

Nilsen, A. G. Forthcoming. *India's Pandemic: Authoritarian Populism and the Politics of a Viral Disaster.* London: Anthem Press.

Ohri, R. 2018. Cow Meat Going Out of India as Carabeef, Police Investigation On. *Economic Times,* 20 March, https://economictimes.indiatimes.com/news/politics-and-nation/cow-meat-going-out-of-india-as-carabeef-police-investigation-on/articleshow/63374600.cms

Paliwal, R. 2022. The Reason Why India can't Ignore Gulf Outrage. *The Economic Times,* 9 June, https://economictimes.indiatimes.com/news/economy/foreign-trade/the-reason-why-india-cant-ignore-gulf-outrage/articleshow/92052158.cms?from=mdr

Press Information Bureau Delhi. 2023. India's Foodgrains Production Touched a Record 315.7 Million Tonnes in 2021–22. 31 January, https://pib.gov.in/PressReleasePage.aspx?PRID=1894899

Processed Food Industry Online. (2020). Recent Aspects of Indian Meat and Meat Products Industry. *Pfionline,* 22 July, https://www.pfionline.com/recent-aspects-of-indian-meat-and-meat-products/

Ramdas, S. R. 2020. Concentration of the Livestock Sector: Through the Lens of Milk and Meat. In *Corporate Concentration in Agriculture and Food,* edited by Premkumar, L., 29–43. N.p: Focus on the Global South, Alternative Law Forum & Rosa Luxemburg Stiftung.

Ramdas, S. R. 2021. India's Deregulated Dairy Sector Signposts the Future of Our Food. *The India Forum,* 30 March, https://www.theindiaforum.in/article/india-s-deregulated-dairy-sector-signposts-future-our-food

Ramdas, S. R. 2023. Livestock Bill Creation and Withdrawal Shows Govt's Disregard for Farmers' Livelihoods. *The Wire,* 22 June, https://thewire.in/government/livestock-bill-creation-and-withdrawal-shows-govts-disregard-for-farmers-livelihoods

Roy, S. 2023. Indian Shoppers to Spend $140–160 Billion Online by 2025: Report. *The Economic Times,* 6 April, https://economictimes.indiatimes.com/tech/technology/indian-shoppers-to-spend-140-160-billion-online-by-2025-report/articleshow/99276263.cms?utm_source=contentofinterest&utm_medium=text&utm_campaign=cppst

Salaria, S. 2022. Black Money Traced, Say IT Officials After Raids on Meat Producers & Exporters in 3 UP Districts. *The Print,* 25 December, https://theprint.in/india/black-money-traced-say-it-officials-after-raids-on-meat-producers-exporters-in-3-up-districts/1281719/

Salve, P. 2020. "Cow Vigilantism has Led to a Major Collapse in Animal Markets and Hurt Farm Incomes": Cattle Expert. *Scroll,* 12 March, https://scroll.in/article/955725/cow-vigilantism-has-led-to-a-major-collapse-in-animal-markets-and-hit-farm-incomes-cattle-expert

Sarkar, S. 2020. India Must Rescue Farmers from Covid-19 Shock. *The Third Pole,* 1 May, https://www.thethirdpole.net/en/food/india-must-rescue-farmers-from-covid-19-shock/

Saxena, Y. 2023. Govt to Combine 2 Mega Dairy Schemes to Help Private Sector. *Krishi Jagran,* 17 April, https://krishijagran.com/news/govt-to-combine-2-mega-dairy-schemes-to-help-private-sector/

Sharma, A. 2022. India, UAE Sign Deal to Boost Trade to $100B by 2027. *AP News,* 18 February, https://apnews.com/article/business-india-united-arab-emirates-global-trade-economy-b72ca1032ca713cd5fe3d3197813f963

Sharma, N. 2020. Frozen is the New Fresh. *The New Indian Express,* 16 July, https://www.newindianexpress.com/lifestyle/food/2020/jul/16/frozen-is-the-new-fresh-2170295.html

Sharma, S. 2020. Modi's "Atmanirbhar Bharat" has Downside Risks Too; will India Take Pre-liberalisation Stand Again? *Financial Express,* 23 September, https://www.financialexpress.com/economy/modis-atmanirbhar-bharat-has-downside-risks-too-will-india-take-pre-liberalisation-stand-again/2089891/

Shivasundar. 2023. Amul-ising KMF: A Ploy to Centralise, Corporatise, and Privatise. *The News Minute,* 17 January, https://www.thenewsminute.com/article/amul-ising-kmf-ploy-centralise-corporatise-and-privatise-172072

Suresh, A. 2016. Consumers' Attitude Towards Meat Consumption in India: Insights from a Survey in Two Metropolitan Cities. *Livestock Research for Rural Development* 28 (3): article 45.

Suwal, L. 2019. Growth Prospects for the Long Unorganized Indian Meat Industry. *Businessworld,* 8 June, https://www.businessworld.in/article/Growth-Prospects-For-The-Long-Unorganized-Indian-Meat-Industry/08-06-2019-171590/

The Hindu. 2022. Make in India, Atmanirbhar Bharat New Definitions of Mahatma Gandhi's Swadeshi Movement: Amit Shah. *The Hindu,* 30 January, https://www.thehindu.com/news/national/make-in-india-atmanirbhar-bharat-new-definitions-of-mahatma-gandhis-swadeshi-movement-amit-shah/article38348932.ece

Tunchum, M. 2022. The India-Middle East Food Corridor: How the UAE, Israel, and India are Forging a New Inter-regional Supply Chain. *The Middle East Institute,* 27 July, https://www.mei.edu/publications/india-middle-east-food-corridor-how-uae-israel-and-india-are-forging-new-inter

Wilhite, H. 2008. *Consumption and the Transformation of Everyday Life: A View from South India.* Basingstoke: Palgrave Macmillan.

Wilhite, H. 2016. *The Political Economy of Low Carbon Transformation: Breaking the Habits of Capitalism.* London: Routledge.

Yadav, L. 2022. How the Frozen Food Industry Giving Tough Competition to Others? *FBNews,* 17 Feburary, http://www.fnbnews.com/Top-News/how-the-frozen-food-industry-giving-tough-competition-to-others-66397

Yadav, P., Khullar, G., Rahman, F., and Farooq, T. 2020. Recent Aspects of Indian Meat and Meat Products Industry. *Processed Food Industry,* 22, July, https://www.pfionline.com/recent-aspects-of-indian-meat-and-meat-products/

5 Concluding Reflections on State Contradictions and Counter-Hegemonic Projects Under Modi's Authoritarian Populism

In a recent contribution to a special issue on authoritarianism and resistance in contemporary India, the esteemed economist Jayati Ghosh (2020) noted how the violent politics of Hindu nationalism and the economics of neoliberalisation appeared to exist in a conflictual relationship under Modi. Ghosh wrote that:

> Several ... elements within the Sangh Parivar, as well as the fringe groups that it periodically disowns even while implicitly encouraging them, have socio-cultural agendas that also affect the economy, often adversely. These agendas are nevertheless privileged and given importance because of the wider social, political and cultural connotations. Thus, for example, *Gau Raksha* ... has turned out to be an unmitigated economic disaster. Not only has *Gau Raksha* attacked the livelihoods (and in some cases lives) of livestock traders (who tend to be disproportionately Muslim or from lower castes), it has also destroyed India's once flourishing beef export industry and the leather industry, which employed lakhs of people. Meanwhile, it has made it uneconomic to hold cattle after they stop being useful for milking which has led to farmers simply releasing cows to forage on their own. The abandoned cattle have thus become a threat to farming itself ... Clearly, this is one aspect of the current manifestation of Hindutva that serves absolutely no economic purpose and does actual material harm.
> (Ghosh 2020)

Ghosh's observation takes us to the heart of the political-economic contradiction that this book has been centrally concerned with, namely that which exists between the socio-cultural agenda of Hindu nationalist politics and the economic agenda of neoliberal restructuring that together constitute Modi's authoritarian populism. Throughout this book, we have analysed this contradiction, which we argue is a key generalised contradiction of the Modi regime, through Poulantzas' idea of state contradictions. This class-analytical approach to the state fruitfully invites consideration of the conjuncturally specific articulations between the "political" and the "economic" that are therefore not considered as distinct realms, but rather as aspects or "moments" of capitalist constellations. This lens has allowed us to scrutinise the ways in which state contradictions in Modi's India play out not merely *within* but more importantly *across* the ostensibly "political" (frequently framed in a "cultural" or "socio-cultural" idiom) and "economic" aspects or moments of Modi's authoritarian populism. Beef and bovine bodies have formed our entry point into the analysis of the playing out of these contradictions because we believe they shine a particularly clear light on them (see also Staples 2020). But the insights derived from this endeavour, we hold, resonate beyond the domain of bovines and bovine political economy. In this concluding chapter, we first briefly summarise the main arguments of the book and specify its contributions to different fields of study. But more importantly, we offer a series of reflections on the implications of our analysis for the future of Modi's authoritarian populism; for thinking about emancipatory strategies aimed at improving the material and political conditions of India's labouring classes; and for strengthening progressive or even counter-hegemonic projects from below at what is arguably a particularly perilous conjuncture in the history of Indian democracy (see Nilsen, Nielsen, and Vaidya 2019). We do so in conversation with the emerging literature on the farmers' movement that unfolded in India from the summer of 2020 onwards, protesting the introduction of new farm laws.

The Political Economy of Modi's Authoritarian Populism

The fact that Modi's authoritarian populism as it currently unfolds rests on the twin pillars of Hindu nationalist cultural politics and neoliberal economic restructuring is widely acknowledged in the literature on contemporary Hindu nationalism. The former pushes an aggressive and chauvinistic form of religious majoritarianism that seeks to turn India into a Hindu state, while the latter seeks to remove obstacles to capitalist accumulation in alignment with dominant class interests. The possible contradictions between the two are, as Ghosh's quote illustrates, often acknowledged, as is Modi's extraordinary capacity for seemingly holding the two together through authoritarian populist measures. And yet it is remarkable how often the crucial political-economic dimension of the Modi regime, and of contemporary Hindu nationalism more generally, tends to disappear from the analysis. Without wishing to single out anyone for negative attention, we note, for example, that Anderson and Longkumer's (2021) influential writings on "neo-Hindutva" in the 21st century do not include issues of political economy or the role of business in the list of questions that effectively constitutes their new research agenda on Hindutva today (ibid.: 2). Jaffrelot's (2021) magisterial book on Modi's rise and consolidation within Indian politics similarly tends to shy away from a more substantial engagement with questions of political economy, which only appear "discretely" (Jaffrelot 2021: 459) in the analysis. While there are very good pragmatic reasons for such analytical backgrounding of the economic "moment" of the Modi regime, or for separating the economic from its political counterpart – having to do with the lack of reliable and publicly available information, and "the secretive political economy of the regime" (Jaffrelot 2021: 459) more generally – we hope our analysis has illustrated what can be gained by insisting on studying the conjuncturally specific articulations between the two.

Pursuing this agenda in the domain of bovine politics and economics, our analysis proceeded from a mapping of a central state contradiction between the socio-political Hindutva "moment" of Modi's authoritarian populism and its intertwined neoliberalising economic "moment" in Chapter 2. Legal and extra-legal cow protectionism has emerged as key aspects of the political landscape under Modi's authoritarian populism to advance the socio-political project of turning India into a Hindu state. This state-supported – sometimes tacitly, sometimes overtly – crackdown on many aspects of the bovine economy, however, has been paralleled in a contradictory way by a dramatic surge in beef exports. Scrutinising this state contradiction by unpacking the political economy of the Indian beef agro-industry, we found an unfolding process of profound sectoral restructuring propelled by Modi's neoliberal economic policies. This process sees an informal bovine economy largely in the hands of classes of labour in the countryside facing aggressive usurping competition from a rising capital intensive formal agro-industry firmly controlled by dominant class interests, sitting in uneasy yet intimate proximity to Modi's regime.

Subsequent chapters traced the consequences of this process and its unfolding dynamics for India's classes of labour partaking in the bovine economy in both countryside and city, clearly documenting the destructive effects on the lives and livelihoods of India's classes of labour. While the immiseration of Muslim workers in, for example, the cattle transportation, meat, and leather sectors that followed from this of course aligns unproblematically with the political moment of Hindu nationalism, the destructive consequences and material harm have impacted classes of labour in the bovine economy much more widely, including cattle owners, dairy farmers, and labourers from low or backward Hindu castes. The last chapter documented an intensification of this process immediately prior to, during, and after the COVID-19 pandemic. This process has thrown the informal bovine economy into a more prolonged crisis while simultaneously enabling the corporate sector to consolidate and capture an increasing share of the bovine wealth that had hitherto been retained among, and been central to the social reproduction of, classes of labour. This gives us reason to be sceptical about Ghosh's (2020) concluding remark that "the current manifestation of Hindutva ... serves absolutely no economic purpose". On our reading, the material consequences documented in this book clearly allow us to deduce if not a purpose, then at least a rationale:

The violent destruction of sectors of the informal bovine economy were a precondition for opening these sectors for greater corporate takeover, in turn, producing greater corporate concentration around dominant class interests in alignment with the overall neoliberal underpinnings of Modi's authoritarian populism.

A brief glance beyond the domain of bovine political economy lends support to our proposition that the contradictions and dynamics we have analysed are exemplary of more generalised political-economic dynamics under Modi. The controversy over three new farm laws that unfolded in India from the summer of 2020 provides a particularly acute and illustrative example of this. Initially introduced as ordinances in June 2020, three agricultural bills were passed into law by the Indian Lok Sabha in September the same year:[1] The Farmers' Produce Trade and Commerce (Promotion and Facilitation) Bill 2020; The Farmers (Empowerment and Protection) Agreement of Price Assurance and Farm Services Bill 2020; and The Essential Commodities (Amendment) Bill 2020. Modi was a strong proponent of these bills which, in his words, would "ensure a complete transformation of the agriculture sector as well as empower crores of farmers". Stressing that his government was there to serve the country's farmers, Modi emphasised how the new laws would "add impetus to the efforts to double the income of farmers and ensure greater prosperity for them". This has been a longstanding promise in Modi's populist efforts to position himself as the champion of Indian farmers, including small, marginal, and distress-hit farmers, the incorporation of whom has been important to the hegemonic and electoral consolidation of Hindu nationalism under Modi. Yet while the political rhetoric surrounding the introduction of the farm laws was strongly pro-poor and centred on the empowerment and "liberation" of marginal and small farmers (or rural classes of labour in our vocabulary) from the shackles of corrupt middlemen and stifling state regulations, the laws themselves were decidedly neoliberal in orientation and expressive of dominant class interests in the agri-business sector (Singh, Singh, and Dhanda 2021). Among other things, they enabled private actors such as supermarket chains, agricultural businesses, and online grocers to deal directly with farmers, enabled speculative hoarding, undermined assured floor prices, and exposed resource-poor and indebted farmers to the full vagaries of market forces. This clear neoliberal tilt was in large measure the result of the secretive work and crucial policy input of a NITI Ayog-appointed task force which served as a platform primarily for big corporate houses involved in agriculture commodities trade, such as the Adani Group, Patanjali, BigBasket, Mahindra Group, and ITC (Jalihal 2023a, 2023b).

That the implementation of these laws would herald entirely new accumulation patterns in agriculture was soon recognised by many Indian farmers' associations and unions who, as we elaborate below, embarked on what was to become the largest and most impactful farmers' movement in decades. While the movement was eventually successful in leading to the repeal of the three laws, what is important for the present discussion is how the protesting farmers were soon exposed to the full authoritarian populist repertoire of Hindu nationalist cultural politics by the Modi regime and allied Hindu nationalist organisations: Protesting farmers marching on Delhi were met with water cannons and tear gas by the police and subject to surveillance by drone cameras; tens of thousands were arrested, with many detained under draconian anti-terrorism laws and charged with anti-national acts of sedition. And in at least one instance, violence was unleashed on farmers when hundreds of vigilantes from the Hindu Sena, a Hindu nationalist group, descended on a protest camp, throwing stones at the protesters, and tearing up their tents. Stigmatised as anti-national enemies out to undermine the Hindu nation, the farmers were branded, through the BJP's hundreds of thousands of WhatsApp groups and its several thousand fake social media handles, as Pakistan-sponsored Khalistani separatists seeking to defame and destabilise India; or as handmaidens of Leftist and Maoist groups fomenting unrest (Nielsen and Nilsen in press; Nielsen and Jakobsen forthcoming). Comparable measures have been used against other actors and groups protesting Modi's neoliberal policies such as environmental activists and land defenders, who are routinely accused of conspiring against India and undermining its national and economic greatness (Dutta and Nielsen 2022). As indicated, this is entirely in line with the grammar of the political moment of Modi's authoritarian populism, which is predicated on imagined fault lines between an authentic Indian people and their antagonistic Other. It also illustrates how an aggressive Hindu nationalist cultural politics can effectively be harnessed to advance neoliberal logics, pointing to a narrowing contradiction between the political and economic moments of Modi's authoritarian populism. A narrowing that is similarly evident in our analysis of bovine political economy in Modi's India, especially in recent years.

Rather than posing the question as being about the extent to which the current manifestation of Hindutva in Modi's India makes economic sense, then, one may ask about the extent to which it makes political sense. Or, to phrase it differently and through the lens of the Hindu nationalist hegemonic project: To what extent is the crucial incorporation of India's poor and working classes politically feasible when it has to occur under conditions that destroy key parts of the livelihoods of these groups? As Jayati Ghosh (2020) asks in the conclusion to her article that we cited at the beginning of this chapter: How far can this strategy be taken? "Can the government continue to mislead and distract people with religious nationalism, or would a collapsing economy and declining livelihoods ultimately also affect the political appeal of Hindutva?" These questions bring us back to the literature on authoritarian populism and the rural world as articulated through the Emancipatory Rural Politics Initiative; and to the issue of how to strengthen counter-hegemonic forces and emancipatory strategies in the context of well-entrenched but nonetheless challenged authoritarian populist rule.

Authoritarian Populism and Counter-Hegemonic Projects

An underlying ambition of this book's analysis of the contentious role of bovine meat in Modi's India has been to connect the Indian experience to the recent attempts arising from the Emancipatory Rural Politics Initiative at understanding the relationship between authoritarian populisms and the rural world more generally. In doing so, we have insisted on going beyond a purely discursive approach to authoritarian populism to engage with "forms and processes of accumulation, class dynamics, and the nature and role of the state" (Mckay et al. 2020: 354). An underlying but only implicitly stated aim has been an increased engagement with state theory. As Vergara-Camus and Kay (2017: 242) have pointed out, much scholarship in critical agrarian studies has highlighted the central role that the state plays in processes of agrarian change. However, very few studies have attempted to re-examine the ways in which we understand the state or have scrutinised the underlying assumptions about the nature of the state that agrarian scholars reproduce. In grappling with this, we have found our Poulantzasian approach and the idea of "internal contradictions within the State" (1978: 131) productive in terms of interrogating some of the otherwise hidden dynamics that may be found in mutually constitutive relation to authoritarian populist projects holding state power. This emphasis on state contradictions within Modi's authoritarian populism has, in particular, enabled us to unpack distinct class and accumulation dynamics between the class coalition supporting Hindutva (especially in the "core" northern states), and the corporate interests behind India's beef export sector.

Despite the subdued optimism with which we concluded the previous section, the prospects for the emergence of counter-hegemonic projects articulating emancipatory strategies at first glance seem bleak. In most respects, Modi's regime does not appear to suffer any serious political consequences from unfolding state contradictions and their detrimental impact on classes of labour. The state elections held in the politically crucial state of Uttar Pradesh in the early months of 2022 bring this out clearly: Despite the efforts of social movements and the political opposition to make the stray cattle problem, the challenge of unemployment, and the controversial farm laws central issues during the campaign, the incumbent Yogi Adityanath government retained a vote share of well over 40 percent and a comfortable (albeit slightly reduced) majority in the state assembly. This durability of Modi's authoritarian populism is no doubt attributable to the fact that its adverse impacts largely affect poorer groups – including Muslims and Dalits – that are unable to threaten his government politically and electorally. And indeed, political support for Modi and the Hindutva cause has overall *increased* among the very groups experiencing double victimisation over the period analysed in this book, albeit unevenly. This mirrors broader political dynamics in contemporary India, where the hegemonic qualities of Modi's authoritarian populism are evident in the impressive ability to continuously incorporate new social groups, including those that are marginalised by Hindu nationalist politics, thus impeding the potential for counter-hegemonic mobilisation. In this regard, the prospects for an emancipatory or counter-hegemonic rural politics are not necessarily strengthened merely by the existence of state contradictions. Studying state contradictions as a way of understanding the relationship between authoritarian populism and the rural world, then, may therefore tell us a good deal more about how authoritarian populism is *made* than how it is to be *unmade*.

An additional factor that makes it, in Borras' (2020) words, "absurdly difficult" to imagine ways in which India's agrarian world could "split the ranks" of Modi's authoritarian populism is the way in which this political project entrenches social fault lines among India's rural classes of labour that seriously hinder the development of oppositional collective action from below. On the one hand, Modi's authoritarian populism is predicated on defining India's Muslim minority as the anti-national enemy within, thus ideologically pitting Muslims against Hindus of all castes. On the other hand, it is predicated on offering the aspirational and moderately upwardly mobile neo-middle classes predominantly from backward caste backgrounds an organic passage into the middle-class mainstream where Hindutva is on a strong footing (Jaffrelot 2015). Although this may happen in a multitude of ways, it often reinforces caste antagonisms between backward castes and Dalits. An emancipatory political project would therefore need to work against these multiple entrenched social fault lines that split the ranks of rural classes of labour. Indeed, as recent contributions to the Emancipatory Rural Politics Initiative also point out with marked emphasis (Borras 2023), it would need to go beyond the "rural" or "agrarian" in isolation – no longer, if ever, reflective of social realities in India or elsewhere – to work towards alliances among classes of labour more broadly.

In this context, we find it useful to begin from Borras's (2020) arguments for a (potential) "left-wing populism" that may work against such entrenched social fault lines, without pretending that they do not exist. The combination of class politics and populism, Borras argues, is desirable *despite* all the tensions and contradictions this combination internalises (ibid.: 28). Such left-wing populism certainly appears as a politico-theoretical landscape of urgent importance, but given its numerous and partly familiar pitfalls, we suggest to slightly more parsimoniously think with Pattenden and Bansal's (2021) recent attempt at grappling with the possibility for new "alliances of classes of labour" to emerge in rural India. When reframed in this way, the prospects

Concluding Reflections 91

are not entirely bleak. As Vanaik (cited in Borras 2020: 24) reminds us, basic agrarian issues continue to render Modi politically vulnerable, as seen recently in the massive farmers' protests against the neoliberalisation of Indian agriculture that we discussed above. Classes of labour, as we have seen, have increasingly taken on a combination of livelihoods, comprising of both farming and wage labour, in efforts that can be seen as seeking forms of "exit" from a sinking agrarian economy. And yet, India's overall political-economic trajectory over the last decades reveals that such an "exit" remains, for most rural Indians, an unobtainable dream. More often than not, households continue to remain dependent in part upon the agrarian base – the vastly diminishing, yet somehow stubbornly persistent income deriving from the land and its yield – for their reproduction. Consequently, as contributions that have assessed the underlying dynamics and significance of the farm law movement have also pointed out (see Baviskar and Levien 2021; Kumar 2022; Lerche 2021), class interests are taking on novel forms of alignment. Writing with specific reference to the perceived disruptions caused by the farm laws, Lerche (2021: 1383) thus asserts that "the different classes of farmers and farmer-labourers have different class interests in many respects, but when it comes to the farm laws, they are united by the fact that they all stand to lose". It is not, however, as *farmers* per se that they stand to lose, but as members of the variegated classes of labour, enmeshed in a vastly complex economy straddling the rural and the urban, and experiencing a "multipronged squeeze" in the neoliberalising political economy (Baviskar and Levien 2021).

Echoing Lerche's assertion, Pattenden and Bansal (2021: 22–23) argue that the farm law protests index several important things about India's contemporary agrarian world, namely (1) that the economic concerns of labourers, farmer-labourers and smaller farmers increasingly overlap; (2) that contradictions *within* the Indian countryside can, to a certain extent and under specific circumstances, be eclipsed by contradictions *beyond* the countryside; and (3) that structurally speaking the Indian countryside is well set for a broad alliance of less wealthy sections. Even if a "new alliance of classes of labour" is unlikely to keep transnational capital and Hindutva politics at bay for now, the vision of their future decline may well be crystallising, Pattenden and Bansal conclude (ibid.: 28; see also Kumar 2021). Further scholarly assessments of the farm law movement lend credence to these propositions. Writing on the movement as it unfolded in Punjab, Singh, Singh, and Dhanda (2021: 12) – while acknowledging that the "political or class character of the movement as a whole is hard to pin down" (ibid.: 12) – describe it as having a "complex cross-caste multi-regional character" with a considerable cadre of landless labourers and women (ibid.:13). Punjab's Left-wing unions working to forge and promote shared interests among smallholders and labourers have been particularly involved (ibid.: 14). The presence of rural wage labourers, most of whom are Dalit, is a particularly clear indication of active cross-class and cross-caste alliances insofar as Punjab's small and medium middle-caste Jat farmers undergoing "unrelenting depeasantisation" (ibid.: 15) and a loss of autonomy over land has often been seen as central to the farm law movement. Importantly, the fact that most rural wage labourers in Punjab are *not* agricultural labourers but mostly make a living in different sectors and across the urban-rural divide also index a possible push beyond the agrarian (see also Jodhka 2021). Moving to western Uttar Pradesh and Haryana – also strongholds of the farm law movement – Kumar (2021) in a comparable manner highlights the resurgence of an encompassing and mobilising "farmer identity" powerful enough to subordinate Hindu-Muslim differences, bringing together Muslim and Jat Hindu farmers on a common political platform. For the movement as a whole, Sandhu (2021) speaks not just of new alliances, but of new solidarities.

Although virtually all assessments of the farm law movement remain sceptical about the depth and durability of such broad alliances or solidarities (e.g. Lerche 2021; Singh 2022), the analyses above at the very least invite us to speculate about the prospects of rural classes of labour forging new alliances around the restructuring bovine economy that this book has analysed. As indicated through our analysis of double victimisation, rural classes of labour among both Dalits and Muslims experience profound adversity, produced at the intersection of religious majoritarianism, ascriptive hierarchies, and class relations. This victimisation and adversity has widened and deepened under Modi's last few years in power by way of the pernicious effects of the COVID-19 lockdown (Nilsen 2022), including – as this book has documented in the realm of bovines – the specific ways COVID-19 has enabled an intensification in corporate capital takeover, leading to spiralling suffering amongst classes of labour in countryside and city. To some extent, albeit only partially, Dalit and Muslims classes of labour share this experience with backward caste small farmers, whose livelihoods have similarly been severely undermined by Modi's bovine politics and economics; and perhaps even with farmers of all size for whom the stray cattle menace has led to significant destruction of crops. Paralleling dynamics embedded in the farm laws in certain respects, then, the concerted and accelerating restructuring of the bovine economy towards the interests of corporate capital may seem to place a broad section of rural social groups in a position where all stand to lose.

In addition, as our analysis has shown, the restructuring of the bovine economy imperils the livelihoods of a very significant number of people embroiled in occupations downstream of livestock rearing – in the slaughter and post-slaughter economy – such that the sections of classes of labour affected in effect crisscross ostensible rural-urban divides. Insofar as these dynamics are becoming increasingly visible and more acutely felt, we have argued that the bovine "lens" on the political economy of Modi's India offered in this book reveals growing cracks – with potentially destabilising ramifications – in Modi's authoritarian populism.

In this regard, our analysis provides some support for Pattenden and Bansal's assertion that the *conditions* are, structurally speaking, well set for a (relatively) broad alliance of "less wealthy sections". More specifically, those who are structurally positioned to forge such an alliance would include Dalits, Muslims, and lower backward castes. Numerous and very significant obstacles to the realisation of such alliances of course remain: Dalit, Muslim, and OBC communities are internally stratified categories who seldom act in uniform ways, neither socially nor politically; the political Hindutva moment of Modi's authoritarian populism works in fragmenting ways by persuasively holding out the prospect of inclusion into a unified sense of Hinduness for Dalits and OBCs and the partial incorporation of some of their aspirations and interests while simultaneously undermining any form of Muslim political engagement; electorally and strategically, the BJP very effectively relies upon a detailed caste arithmetic (with fragmenting effects) in appealing specifically to those Dalit and Backward castes that feel marginalised by broader attempts at lower caste assertion in the domain of electoral politics; and of course, lower OBC communities cannot automatically be expected to look "downwards for alliances rather than upwards" (Pattenden and Bansal 2021: 21–22, 28). To this we can add the usual perils and pitfalls involved in forging cross-caste, cross-class alliances (Nielsen 2016, 2018; Pattenden 2016). Contentions surrounding the cattle economy will therefore not in their own right bring such alliances into being, and the actual formation of new alliances for progressive counter-mobilisation will still depend on "how the class dynamics of capitalism play out in various countrysides", and the extent to which those dynamics generate more or less clear class categories that manifest in distinct forms of political practice (Bernstein 2020: 1533). Furthermore, as recently articulated by Borras (2023), the formation of "alliances" in broad, generic terms is only the beginning: "The operational challenge", Borras (2023: 458) writes, "is how to translate amorphous notions of class alliances into something tangible and workable in politico-organizational terms".

Nonetheless, we would reiterate, the objective conditions surrounding the country's classes of labour may at the very least index political possibility and potential. In other words, the ways in which Modi's authoritarian populism is reconfiguring India's bovine economy may open up and make visible new spaces for progressive, and perhaps even counter-hegemonic mobilisation, starting from locations of profound adversity that are configured in such a way that they break with the very social fault lines that undergird and sustain Modi's authoritarian populism. How such possibility and potential will play out, and the extent to which we will see counter-hegemonic tendencies crystallising in tangible organisational forms, will, as always, be determined in and through political struggle.

Evidently, this opens for recurring, thorny "politico-organisational" questions about the possible conjunction of new alliances of classes of labour and the more established Left, including in the shape of trade union mobilisation.

94 Concluding Reflections

Witnessing the seemingly increased capacity of Leftist trade unions at sustaining and perhaps even strengthening the reach of alliances of classes of labour in the context of the 2020–2021 farm law protests, such thorny issues may not be without promise. As Poulantzas (2017) put it shortly before his passing, revealing an optimism of the will that can speak to our concerns, conjunctions between popular mobilisation and the organised Left are defined by "a certain irreducible tension" – yet this tension, Poulantzas suggests, is likely "an integral part" of progressive political transformation. A future research agenda capable of interrogating authoritarian populism *and* thinking through emancipatory strategies from below would, by implication, have to carefully trace actual processes of accumulation and class formation; engage and unpack the state and state contradictions in context-specific ways; and work towards a detailed disaggregation of local class relations to identify those social locations of extreme adversity from which counter-hegemonic projects might emerge.

Note

1 An ordinance is equivalent to a law passed by parliament (but with limited duration) but does not involve parliament. Rather, the President of India passes the law on the recommendation of the Union cabinet. Ordinances are, in principle, to be used when parliament is not in session and an emergency requires that the government makes changes to existing legislation or brings in new legislation to deal with the situation. But in practice ordinances have for more than half a century been frequently used by shifting Indian governments to bypass parliament and evade parliamentary debate on controversial policy issues.

References

Anderson, E., and Longkumer, A. 2021. Introduction – "Neo-Hindutva": Evolving Forms, Spaces, and Expressions of Hindu Nationalism. In *Neo-Hindutva: Evolving Forms, Spaces, and Expressions of Hindu Nationalism*, edited by Anderson, E., and Longkumer, A., 1–8. London: Routledge.

Baviskar, A., and Levien, M. 2021. Farmers' Protests in India: Introduction to the JPS Forum. *Journal of Peasant Studies* 48 (7): 1341–1355.

Bernstein, H. 2020. Unpacking "Authoritarian Populism" and Rural Politics: Some Comments on ERPI. *Journal of Peasant Studies* 47 (7): 1526–1542.

Borras, S. M. 2020. Agrarian Social Movements: The Absurdly Difficult but Not Impossible Agenda of Defeating Right-Wing Populism and Exploring a Socialist Future. *Journal of Agrarian Change* 20 (1): 3–36.

Borras, S. M. 2023. Contemporary Agrarian, Rural and Rural–urban Movements and Alliances. *Journal of Agrarian Change* 23 (3): 453–476.

Dutta, A., and Nielsen, K. B. 2022. The Autocratization of Environmental Governance in India. In *Routledge Handbook on Autocratization in South Asia*, edited by Widmalm, S., 70–80. London: Routledge.

Ghosh, J. 2020. Hindutva, Economic Neoliberalism and the Abuse of Economic Statistics in India. *Samaj* 24/25: 1–8.

Jaffrelot, C. 2015. The Class Element in the 2014 Indian Election and the BJP's Success with Special Reference to the Hindu Belt. *Studies in Indian Politics* 3 (1): 19–38.

Jaffrelot, C. 2021. *Modi's India: Hindu Nationalism and the Rise of Ethnic Democracy*. Princeton, NJ: Princeton University Press.

Jalihal, S. 2023a. Ahead of Farm Laws, an NRI Seeded Idea to Corporatise Agriculture. *The Reporters' Collective*, 16 August, https://www.reporters-collective.in/trc/ahead-of-farm-laws-an-nri-seeded-idea-to-corporatise-agriculture

Jalihal, S. 2023b. Adani Group Complained Against Farm Law. Gov't Diluted it to Allow Hoarding by Corporates. *The Reporters' Collective*, 16 August, https://www.reporters-collective.in/trc/adani-group-complained-against-farm-law-govt-diluted-it-to-allow-hoarding-by-corporates

Jodhka, S. S. 2021. Why Are the Farmers of Punjab Protesting? *Journal of Peasant Studies* 48 (7): 1356–1370.

Kumar, S. 2021. Class, Caste and Agrarian Change: The Making of Farmers' Protests. *Journal of Peasant Studies* 48 (7): 1371–1379.

Kumar, S. 2022. New Farm Bills and Farmers' Resistance to Neoliberalism. *Sociological Bulletin* 71 (4): 483–494.

Lerche, J. 2021. The Farm Laws Struggle 2020–2021: Class-caste Alliances and Bypassed Agrarian Transition in Neoliberal India. *Journal of Peasant Studies* 48 (7): 1380–1396.

McKay, B. M., Oliveira, G. de L. T., and Liu, J. 2020. Authoritarianism, Populism, Nationalism and Resistance in the Agrarian South. *Canadian Journal of Development Studies / Revue Canadienne d'études du Développement* 41 (3): 347–362.

Nielsen, K. B. 2016. The Politics of Caste and Class in Singur's Anti-Land Acquisition Struggle. In *The Politics of Caste in West Bengal*, edited by Chandra, U., Heierstad, G. and Nielsen, K. B., 125–146. New Delhi: Routledge.

Nielsen, K. B. 2018. *Land Dispossession and Everyday Politics in Rural Eastern India*. London: Anthem Press.

Nielsen, K. B., and Jakobsen, J. Forthcoming. Food Politics and Hindu Nationalist Statecraft. In *Cambridge Companion to Indian Politics and Society*, edited by Roy, I. and Desai, M. Cambridge: Cambridge University Press.

Nielsen, K. B., and Nilsen, A. G. In press. The Kisan Andolan and India's Roll-over Neoliberalism. In *Exploring the Kisan Andolan: Agrarian Crisis, Dissent and Identity*, edited by Singh, D. and Moliner, C. New Delhi: Routledge.

Nilsen, A. G. 2022. India's Pandemic: Spectacle, Social Murder and Authoritarian Politics in a Lockdown Nation. *Globalizations* 19 (3): 466–486.

Nilsen, A. G., Nielsen, K. B., and Vaidya, A. (eds) 2019. *Indian Democracy: Origins, Trajectories, Contestations*. London: Pluto Press.

Pattenden, J. 2016. *Labour, State and Society in Rural India: A Class-Relational Approach*. Manchester: Manchester University Press.

Pattenden, J., and Bansal, G. 2021. A New Class Alliance in the Indian Countryside? From New Farmers' Movements to the 2020 Protest Wave. *Economic and Political Weekly* 56 (26/27): 22–29.

Poulantzas, N. 1978. *State, Power, Socialism*. London: New Left Review Editions.

Poulantzas, N. 2017 (1979). The State, Social Movements, Party: Interview with Nicos Poulantzas (1979). *Viewpoint Magazine*, 18 December, https://viewpointmag.com/2017/12/18/state-social-movements-party-interview-nicos-poulantzas-1979/

Sandhu, A. 2021. Left, Khaps, Gender, Caste: The Solidarities Propping up the Farmers' Protest. *Caravan*, 13 January, https://caravanmagazine.in/agriculture/left-punjab-haryana-caste-gender-solidarities-farmers-protest

Singh, S. 2022. *Khaps* in the Making of Farmers' Protests in Haryana: A Study of Role and Fault Lines. *Sociological Bulletin* 71 (4): 534–550.

Singh, T., Singh, P., and Dhanda, M. 2021. Resisting a "Digital Green Revolution": Agri-Logistics, India's New Farm Laws and the Regional Politics of Protest. *Capitalism Nature Socialism* 32 (2): 1–21.

Staples, J. 2020. *Sacred Cows and Chicken Manchurian: The Everyday Politics of Eating Meat in India*. Seattle: University of Washington Press.

Vergara-Camus, L., and Kay, C. 2017. Agribusiness, Peasants, Left-Wing Governments, and the State in Latin America: An Overview and Theoretical Reflections. *Journal of Agrarian Change* 17 (2): 239–257.

Index

Note: *Italic* page numbers refer to figures and page numbers followed by "n" denote endnotes.

accumulation: capital 2, 3, 9, 24, 33, 35, 40; dynamics 9, 15, 16, 35, 65, 66, 73, 76, 77, 80, 89; patterns 9, 15, 35–38, 87
actors 2, 4, 17, 37, 67, 88
Adityanath, Yogi 18, 30, 56, 89
agrarian change 17, 39, 46, 89
Agricultural and Processed Food Products Export Development Authority (APEDA) 1–2, 37
agriculture 4, 54, 75–76, 87; and allied activities 4; commodities trade 87; economy 49; and food production 75; global markets and value chains 3; labourers 13, 47, 92; neoliberalisation 91; products 2, 75; transformation of 87
Ahmad, Zarin 37, 51
Akhil Bharatiya Vidyarthi Parishad 31, 33
Alam, Afroz 46
Alavi, Fauzan 39, 77–78
Al Dua Food Processing Pvt Ltd. 38
Al-Hamd Agro Foods Products Pvt. Ltd. 2, 66
Allanasons Pvt. Ltd. 1–2, 37
Anand Milk Union Limited (Amul) 76
Anderson, E. 85
Andhra Pradesh 37, 57, 71; beef export processing units 37; beef festivals 33; *gaushalas* institution 57; water buffalo populations 71

Animal Husbandry Infrastructure Development Fund (AHIDF) 76, 78
Animal Intimacies: Interspecies Relatedness in India's Central Himalayas (Govindrajan) 5
Animal Welfare Board of India 57
anti-Muslim: controversies in India 72; sentiments, contemporary cow vigilantism 32
Arya, Manjeet 24
anti-national enemies 24, 33, 88, 90
Assam 52–53
Atma Nirbhar Bharat Abhiyaan 66, 75, 77, 78
authoritarian populism 2, 5–9, 11, 89–94; authoritarian statism 8; bovine paradox 3, 5; bovine politics and economics 4, 47, 49; capital accumulation and class 40; central state contradictions 15; class contradictions and antagonisms 8; counter-hegemonic projects 89; cow vigilantism 40; definition of 24; economic moments of 7, 66, 80, 85; hegemonic qualities of 90; Hindu nationalist politics 8; ideological and discursive qualities of 8; impact on rural classes of labour 17; neoliberalisation, economic moment of 59; political moment 24, 65, 88; rural societies

7; socio-political Hindutva moment 25, 39, 86; state-capital relations 13; state contradictions 89; *see also* Modi, Narendra; *individual entries*
Bangladesh 13, 52, 71
Bansal, G. 90
beef: agro-industry 18, 35, 80; bans 5, 50; corporate beef export industry 3; criminalisation 51; Dalit Hindus and Muslims 25; detection kits 32; exports 3, 6, 33, 34, 37, 38, 40, 65, 66, 70–73, 78, 86, 89; festivals 33; Hindu right-wing groups 5; hyper-politicization of 5; indirect beef ban 41n4; milk-and-beef economy 36; post-pandemic beef exports 71; trade 65, 68; *see also individual entries*
Bernstein, H. 8, 40, 46
Bharatiya Janata Party (BJP) 2, 5; beef export industry 38; Bharatiya Jan Sangh 28; caste arithmetic 93; cow protection 29; economic liberalisation 9; economic neoliberalism 11; election campaign 39–40; hegemonic strategy 13, 24; Hindu nationalist project 41n4; Hindu right-wing groups 5; India Shining campaign 10, 12; neoliberal reforms 6; political Hindu nationalism 11; rights-based welfare 10; Vajpayee government 28; *see also* Rashtriya Swayamsevak Sangh (RSS)
Bharatiya Kisan Sangh 77
Bolsonaro, Jair 6
Bombay Mutton Dealers' Association 49
Borras, S. M. 90, 93
Bovine Politics in South Asia: Rethinking Religion, Law and Ethics (Adcock and Govindrajan) 5
Brahmanism 57
buffalo meat exports 2, 25, *34*
capital: accumulation 2, 3, 9, 24, 33, 35, 40; agro-industrial sectors 39, 86; bovine economy 24; capital-labour relation 9; class antagonism of 9; and class dynamics 14; corporate capital 4, 66, 92; and Hindutva politics 91; labour relation 9; pro-capital economic 19n6; state-capital relations 12, 38
capitalism 9, 13, 93
capitalist: accumulation 6, 85; classes, benefit 16; cultural nationalism 12; dynamics 3, 8; enterprises 36; growth 12; post-slaughter economies 70
cattle/cow/bovine: agricultural economy 49; agro-industry 33–40, 37, 58; care camps 58; cow protectionism 40; economy 3, 4, 16, 33–40, 35, 46, 48–55, 49, 66, 86, 93; female cattle 48; Hindu nationalist politics 40; human interactions with 66; illegal cattle trading 55; informal bovine economy 40, 86; lumpy skin disease 72; markets 50, 55; Modi's authoritarian populism 49; natural death 34; paradox 3, 4, 5–9, 8; political economy 4, 15, 18; politics 3, 24, 27; post-slaughter economy 51; smugglers 53; state-capital relations 38; stray cattle menace 56; symbolism 15, 24, 25–27; transportation 2; *see also* protection, cow; *individual entries*
Chancel, L. 9
Chatterjee, E. 13
Clarke, S. 9
class: accumulation dynamics 35, 65, 76; analytical approach 8–9, 84; antagonism of capital and labour 9; authoritarian populism 8; capital accumulation 35; cross-class alliances 93; dynamics 8, 13–14, 24, 35, 89, 93; Hindu voters 14; and intra-class relationships 8; state-capital relations 14
classes of labour 3, 4, 6, 10, 13, 14, 15, 33, 35, 46, 55, 70; in bovine economy 86; broad category of 49; concept of 47; double victimisation of 16; Hindu

Index

nationalist support 14; and militant protectionism 32; negative impact on 53; rural classes of labour 6–7, 17–18, 35, 48–50, 53–54, 56–58, 70, 87, 90, 92; social division of 47
"conglomerate" capitalism 13
contemporary Hindu nationalism 17, 24, 85
contemporary India 7, 9, 17, 46–47, 84, 90
The Conversation (Alam) 46
corporate: agricultural exports 2; beef export industry 3; bovine meat sector 35; concentration 3, 35, 65–80, 87; food sector/industry 73, 75; frozen meat products 68; pro-corporate design 76; socialism 10; social responsibility 18
counter-hegemonic: identity 33; mobilisation 4, 16, 47, 90, 93; projects 16, 88, 89–94; rural politics 90
COVID-19 pandemic 47, 66, 68, 73, 86
cultural politics 2, 12, 85, 88

Dairy Processing and Infrastructure Development Fund 76
Dalits 13, 14, 25, 32, 33, 46, 49, 52, 54, 59, 89–91, 93
Dhanda, M. 91
domestic consumption 35, 55, 72, 74
domestic beef markets 37, 67, 69, 76
domestic market 37, 67, 69
double victimisation 4, 15, 16, 18, 46–60, 80, 90, 92
Duterte, Rodrigo 6

Echeverri-Gent, J. 4
economics 4, 8–9, 17, 24, 46–47, 49, 66, 80, 84–86, 92; authoritarian populism 7; capital accumulation 3; classes of labour 4; COVID-19 pandemic 16; cow economics 46; growth and liberalisation 28; inequality 18n3; instability and vulnerability 13, 14; liberalisation 9; Modi government 2, 65; Muslim classes of labour 7; neoliberalisation/neoliberalism 11, 59; neoliberal restructuring 3; policies 6, 33, 40, 65, 86; rural classes of labour 56; Vajpayee government 28
2022–2023 Economic Survey 76
Emancipatory Rural Politics Initiative 7, 88, 89, 90
Erdoğan, Recep Tayyip 6
Essential Commodities (Amendment) Bill 2020 87

farmers 26, 36, 47–50, 55–56, 78, 84–85, 87–88, 91–92
Farmers (Empowerment and Protection) Agreement of Price Assurance and Farm Services Bill 2020 87
Farmers' Produce Trade and Commerce (Promotion and Facilitation) Bill 2020 87
farm law movement 91–92
Fischer, J. 5, 73
frozen foods 73–75, 74; COVID-19 pandemic 66, 74; meat products 68

gau rakshaks 24, 30–32, 55
Gau Raksha Manch (cow protection front) 30
gaushalas: initiative 31; maintenance projects 57; political economy of 56–59
Ghosh, Jayati 84, 86, 88
Global South 7, 13, 47
Gopalakrishnan, Shankar 12
government slaughterhouses 53–54, 67–69
Govindrajan, Radhika 5, 26, 60n1
"great all-party campaign" 28
The Guardian 31–32
Gujarat 30, 57; Anand Milk Union Limited 76; *gaushalas,* political economy of 58; vigilante attacks, cattle traders 32

Hall, Stuart 8
Hansen, Thomas Blom 14
Hardy, Kathryn 26
Harriss-White, B. 47
Haryana 29, 41n5, 49, 52–53, 57–59, 92; bovine politics 49; closure of slaughterhouses 53; cow protection commission 57; cow protection legislation 29; farm

law movement 92; *gaushalas* 57; ID-tag for cattle and bovines 53; Muslims, vigilante groups 53
The Hindu 54
Hindu/Hinduism 24, 27; activists and vigilantes 25; administration 52; bovine politics 27, 69; cattle and cattle transporters 32; cow veneration 2; cow vigilantism 4; cultural politics 2, 85; definition of 27; fundamentalists 27; Hindu Sena 88; Hindu state 15, 24, 27, 85; Hindu unity 14, 58; majoritarianism 11; mother cow 57; movement 28, 57, 77; nationalism 5, 11–12, 16, 18, 24–33, 35–40, 59, 78, 84, 86–87; politics 17, 18, 24, 86; rashtra 33; right-wing groups 1, 5, 28; ritual Hinduism 57; ritual purification 25; socio-cultural agenda 3, 84; ultranationalism 3, 57; vigilante violence 2, 66; violent politics of 84; voters 14
Hindu Yuva Vahini (Hindu youth brigade) 30
HMA Agro Industries 66
Human Rights Watch 32, 41n5

illegal cattle trading 55
illiberal cultural nationalism 12
Income Tax department 66
India: agriculture (*see* agriculture); anti-Muslim controversies 72; bovine agro-industry 37; bovine paradox 3, 4; bovine political economy 4, 15; buffalo meat exports 2; capital accumulation 2; classes of labour 13; "conglomerate" capitalism 13; corporate-led agricultural exports 2; cultural heritage 28; dairy and meat industry 6; frozen foods market 74; labouring classes 85; Muslim minority 27, 90; neoliberalisation in 9–10, 12, 15, 33, 59, 84, 91; non-vegetarian dietary traditions 27; rights-based welfare 10; social and cultural diversity 25; soft power 28; *see also individual entries*

"India Shining" campaign 10, 12
India Times 24
informal livestock system 37
Islamophobic gastronomy 33

Jakobsen, J. 41n1
Jaffrelot, C. 18, 85
Jha, D. K. 30
Jha, D. N. 27–28
Jharkhand: cow protection 1; ID-tag for cattle and bovines 53
Joshi, S. 55

Kanpur Municipal Corporation 69
Karnataka: class-specific accumulation dynamics 76; cow protection laws 31, 41n4; Hindutva, laboratories of 18; Prevention of Slaughter and Preservation of Cattle Act, 2020 30, 55; pro-corporate design 76
Karnataka Cooperative Milk Federation (KMF) 76
Karpagam S. 55
Kaur, R. 11
Kay, C. 89
Kerala 75; beef festivals 33
Kothakapa, G. 10, 12
Kumar, S. 92

left-wing populism 90
legal protectionism 24, 33
Lerche, J. 91
licence 53, 68, 69
Livestock and Livestock Products Bill, 2023 77
livestock economy 4, 15, 35, 36
Longkumer, A. 85
long-term sectoral restructuring 68–70
lumpy skin disease 72

macro-economic indicators 13
Madhya Pradesh 48, 58
Maharashtra 29, 37, 48–51, 53–55, 71–72; beef export processing units 37; bovine politics 49; cattle economy 49; cow protection operations 29; Qureshi Muslim community 54; sale of cattle in 51, 72; water buffalo populations 71
"Make in India" programme 19n6, 39, 54
Mander, Harsh 52

Index 101

Mazlum and Imteyaz case 1
McKay, B. M. 8, 40
meat 5, 25, 29, 34–39, 46, 51–52, 66–70, 73–77, 79, 86
Middle East 34, 66–67, 71–72
Modi, Narendra: Atmanirbhar Bharat mission 75, 78; authoritarian populist style 14; bovine politics and economics 66; 2014 campaign 10; corporate-led economic growth 11; double standards 38; *gaushalas* 58; Hindu nationalist government 2, 6; Hindu nationalist movement 31; macro-economic indicators 13; "Make in India" agenda 39, 54; national ban on cow slaughter 29; neoliberal economic policies 40, 65; neoliberalism 9, 12; pink revolution 79; political dynamics 3; political economy 2, 6, 85–89; poverty estimates 13; Rashtriya Swayamsevak Sangh 28; right-wing deepening 46; socio-political Hindutva moment 25; state-capital relations 14; state contradictions 9; *see also* authoritarian populism
Mother Cow, Mother India: A Multispecies Politics of Dairy in India (Narayanan) 6
Mother India 6, 27
municipal slaughterhouses 37, 53–54, 67, 70
Muslims 25, 27, 31, 54, 89; anti-national enemy 33, 90; in cattle trade 40; cattle transporters 32; cow protectionism 2; political emaciation 59; Qureshi community 49; vigilante violence 53
The Myth of the Holy Cow (Jha) 27, 28

Narayanan, Yamini 6, 25, 30, 32, 36, 57
National Green Tribunal 53
National Human Rights Commission 39
National Meat and Poultry Processing Board 34
National Mission for Food Processing 39
National Sample Survey Organisation (NSSO) 47

"neo-Hindutva" 85
neoliberal 9; bovine economy 35; capitalist growth 12; economic agenda of 84; economic policies 3, 6; ideology of 12; restructuring process 10; shock therapy 9; state contradictions 9; and welfare policy 10
Nepal 13, 56
Nielsen, K. B. 9, 41n1
Nilsen, A. G. 9, 14

oligarchic state capitalism 13
organised export-oriented industry 66–68

Palshikar, Suhas 11
Pattenden, J. 90
Piketty, T. 9
Pink Revolution 38, 79
political/politics 2, 12, 85; economy 2–3, 5–6, 8, 12, 17, 35, 37, 40, 57–58, 85–86, 91–92; Hindu nationalism 11; Hindutva moment 33, 39; moment 24; segregation 28–29; sphere 2, 11
populism 7, 90
Poulantzas, Nicos 3, 8, 9
protection, cow 1, 2, 5, 6, 15, 24, 27–29, 30, 33, 41n3; under article 48 29; commission 57; Hindu nationalist ideology of 35; Hindu nationalist project of 5; legislation 26, 29; politicisation 28; protectionists 40; slaughter 28, 29; societies 27; task force 29; universal demand for 25; vigilantism 14, 30, 31, 32, 40, 49
Punjab 92; beef export processing units 37; cross-caste alliances 92; Left-wing unions 91; rural wage labourers 92

Qureshi Muslim community 51, 54

racism 11, 24
Rajasthan 30, 49, 51–53, 58–59, 72; bovine politics 49; cow vigilantes 51; *gaushalas* 58; nomadic-pastoral communities 60n2
Ramdas, S. R. 49, 65
ramifications 3, 7, 15–16, 46, 49

Index

Rashtriya Swayamsevak Sangh (RSS) 28, 31, 77; Hindu nationalist movement 77; Mahatma Gandhi, murder of 28
red revolution 79
rural: classes of labour 48, 56, 57; households 4, 47–48, 51–52; India, bovine economy 4; world 5, 7, 88–90

Sacred Cows and Chicken Manchurian: The Everyday Politics of Eating Meat in India (Staples) 5
Sandhu, A. 92
Shah, A. 47, 76
shakti (divine power) 26
Shivasundar 76, 77
Simhachalam Temple Gaushalas in Andhra Pradesh 57
Singh, P. 91
Singh, T. 91
Sirohi, R. A. 10, 12
slaughterhouses 39, 53, 55, 57, 66, 68–72, 79; *see also individual entries*
socio-political Hindutva "moment" 25, 86
Som, Sangeet 38
Special Economic Zones Act 19n4
Staples, James 2, 5, 25
state contradictions 3–17, 35, 38–39, 66, 78, 80, 84–86, 89–90, 94
supply chains 37, 55, 66, 70–71; disruptions 66
swaraj and *swadeshi* 76

Teotia, Rita 2
Thatcherism 8
trade 39–40, 50, 52, 54, 65, 68, 70–72, 79
transportation 2, 29, 31, 54
true Indians 24, 33
Trump, Donald 6

unemployment 13, 89
United Arab Emirates (UAE) 71, 72

United Progressive Alliance (UPA) 10
UN's Food and Agriculture Organization 34
Urban India 73
Uttar Pradesh 17–18, 30, 37–38, 46, 48–49, 53–56, 58–59, 66–72, 78–79, 89; beef economy in 55; beef export processing units 37; bovine politics 49; cow slaughter, legal punishments 30; farm law movement 92; *gaushalas* in 57; Hindutva, laboratories of 18; slaughterhouse ecology 53; water buffalo populations 71

Vajpayee government: economic growth and liberalisation 28
vegetarianism 5, 27–28, 35
Vegetarianism, Meat and Modernity in India (Fischer) 5
Vergara-Camus, L. 89
Vietnam 34, 39, 71
vigilante groups 18, 24, 29–31, 49, 52–53, 55, 57
vigilantism 15, 30, 52, 59, 69; politics 15, 30–33; cow 31–32, 40, 49, 67
violence 14, 32, 49, 51–52, 56, 88

"wages of violence" 14, 32, 59
waste, corporate sector alignment 77–79
water buffalo detection kits 32–33
welfare programmes 10, 14
West Bengal 52
WhatsApp groups 49, 88
White Revolution 35
Wilhite, H. 75
working classes 2–4, 13–14, 16, 46, 88
World Hindu Council (VHP) 27

xenophobia 11, 24

Yadav caste 26

For Product Safety Concerns and Information please contact our EU
representative GPSR@taylorandfrancis.com
Taylor & Francis Verlag GmbH, Kaufingerstraße 24, 80331 München, Germany

www.ingramcontent.com/pod-product-compliance
Lightning Source LLC
Chambersburg PA
CBHW051757230426
43670CB00012B/2320